THE NAVAHO DOOR

Navaho Mother and Child

The NAVAHO DOOR

AN INTRODUCTION TO NAVAHO LIFE

Alexander H. Leighton
Dorothea C. Leighton

FOREWORD BY JOHN COLLIER, COMMISSIONER OF INDIAN AFFAIRS

NEW YORK / RUSSELL & RUSSELL

Dedicated to the thousands of Navahos in the fighting forces
of the United States

CONTENTS

ILLUSTRATIONS

ACKNOWLEDGMENTS

WE ARE INDEBTED to so many people and organizations for the material used in this book that it is not possible to name them all. Perhaps the first on the list should be Dr. Adolf Meyer of the Johns Hopkins Hospital, whose wisdom and encouragement first led us to study Indian peoples; then the Social Science Research Council, who provided the funds for the year's research when we made the acquaintance of the Navaho; next, Dr. Clyde Kluckhohn of Harvard University, who introduced us to the Navaho and has been helpful in innumerable ways since then.

Of primary importance also are the Navahos we have known, lived with and talked to: Mr. David Skeet and his family; many Ramah and Two Wells Navahos; Mr. Stewart Barton, Miss Myrtle Morris, Mr. Adolf Bitanny, Mr. George Hood, Mrs. Grace McCrae, to name a few.

The staff of the Indian Office and the Navaho Field Service must also be noted, especially Hon. John Collier, the Commissioner, who asked us to write this book; Dr. J. R. McGibony, Jr. and Mr. D'Arcy McNickle, who had charge of many of the arrangements; Mr. L. T. Hoffman, Mr. George Boyce, Mr. Solon Kimball of the Navaho Service administrative staff; Mr. Earl Rains, Mrs. Ruby Tomlinson, Miss Rachel Jordan, Mrs. Lisbeth Eubank, Mr. Seymour Anderson of the teachers; Dr. W. W. Peter, Dr. Leo Schnur, Dr. Eric Johnson, Dr. W. S. Lewis, Miss Geraldine Quinn, Miss Carolyn Conti, Mrs. Talcott, and Mrs. Showalter, of the medical staff.

Much of the material on Navaho religion appeared in our article "Elements of Psychotherapy in Navaho Religion," *Psychiatry* 4: pp. 515-523, 1941. It is reproduced by permission. The quotation from William James's *The Will to Believe, and Other Essays in Popular Philosophy* (Longmans, Green and Co., 1897) is reproduced by permission of the publisher. Helen Post has kindly allowed us to use some of her photographs as illustrations.

Last, but by no means least, our thanks are due to Miss Abra Ella Spicer, who was of great assistance in preparing this manuscript.

All these people and many more have contributed to our understanding of the Navaho Indian and the various problems and successes related to him, as have also many anthropologists, novelists, traders, missionaries, and white ranchers. In this book we have tried to bring together some of their teachings in a way that will be helpful to others in making the acquaintance of the largest group of native Americans in the United States.

A. H. L.
D. C. L.

FOREWORD

FIVE OR SIX YEARS AGO, the headquarters staff of the United States Indian Service listened to Doctors Alexander and Dorothea Leighton, and experienced a deep excitement. There were some who realized that here was a practical utility long waited for, in the particular field of Indian health work. Some others glimpsed a method and a principle of application possibly very wide, bearing upon the problems of culture-groups in many lands. Others, again, were stirred by a deepened vision of the resources of the human psyche and spirit—the psyche and spirit of "primitive" men.

The Leightons, on that occasion, were telling of their research among Navaho Indians. This book is one of the fruits of that research.

Cross-cultural relations are a localized and also a planet-wide laboratory of the soul, though not often treated as such. This laboratory does not yield discovery to the careless inquirer, or to the invader who is moved by unconscious ethnic egotism. Studies must reach deep, and they must be conducted by evolved personalities, if in this laboratory they are to win results either locally or universally valid. The studies of Navaho healing institutions, which are the heart of this book of the Leightons, surely are such deep-reaching instances; and their local, if not their universal, validity is evident at once.

Human cultures inter-act with one another, of necessity. The speed and the promiscuity of these inter-actions, in our day, are increasing all the time. These inter-actions can generate social energy or they can dissipate it and destroy the organs which produce it. They can be the occasion of creative new beginnings, or they can shatter the chances of the future. Multitudinous and speeded-up contacts are leaping from the European-American culture systems to the systems of "primitive," "pre-industrial" peoples. Personality can be built up or broken down through these cross-cultural contacts. In individual and local cases, almost nothing except the meretricious, even the death-dealing effect, may seem to pass from a dominating to a dominated culture. Are prediction, direction, and beneficent control of results possible in this very critical area of the human situation? The answer is not of the all-or-none sort. Through knowledge, through "empathy," through initiative and forbearance alike, it is certain that the course of events in cultural inter-action can be influenced helpfully, at least to some extent. As social science and social art become more adequate, it may be that a preponderating control will be found to lie within the reach of men.

This is the problem which the Leightons commenced to examine in a particular area of the life of one Indian tribe. Bringing to this Navaho community a very competent medical and psychiatric equipment, and sophisticated and sensitive minds, they received the help of one of the most creative-minded of social anthropologists, Dr. Clyde Kluckhohn of Harvard. While the orientation of their project was not less than world-wide, its application involved a transposition of their own stream of consciousness into Navaho Indian experience. They moved into the center of the Navaho's world-view and of his life effort. They made no deductive intrusion. Hence, their results are valid locally and specifically. They are the three-dimensional results, persuasive, dependable, and abiding. Even to one who did not know the Navaho through deep personal experience, the records and the conclusions of the Leightons would have an awakening and a persuading virtue such as Tolstoy's human narratives have. Those who do know the Navahos through deep personal experience find their horizon of Navaho life pushed backward in the most exciting and challenging way. They feel renewed within them the thought of Tennyson's Ulysses: "To follow knowledge like a sinking star beyond the utmost bound."

There is, however, a nearer focus. The discoveries and generalizations of the Leightons, in this Navaho area, have been found usable by the administrator. Their implications are much wider than the area of health work alone. I believe that they would have instant and practical use to administrators faced with challenges and opportunities which are at all similar, and I believe that this may mean nearly all administrators, at least in the "colonial" and "minorities" fields.

So adequate, and so self-completing, is this present book, that I have not easily seen what it might be that a foreword could add to it. Then I recalled, that behind this book were the labors of a concentrated and important thinking concerning body and mind in society, and that this study (like more recent ones by the Leightons in other areas) was done in the light of hypotheses, and toward the development of technics, purposefully relevant to the world's most universal problem and enigma; and that this Navaho case is only a special case, heavy as is its burden of universal life.

This book is meant for Indian Service workers, in the first instance. It will help some of them toward knowing that their work—or at least their opportunity—exists here among the Navaho, upon the watershed of the social world.

JOHN COLLIER
Commissioner of Indian Affairs

INTRODUCTION

IN the stretch of wild country where the states of New Mexico, Arizona, Utah and Colorado meet, there are a few surfaced roads. Touring along one of these one year, we turned from the hard pavement onto a sandy track, and went off across the wide sage-covered plain. We drove for miles without seeing a sign of house or man. Finally, perched beside a windmill on a little hill, we came upon a low, flat-roofed, adobe building with a red gas pump in front. The last pump we had passed was fifty miles away.

Inside was a room with counters and shelves all around, and a tan-faced, wind-blown man in a big hat, going over his accounts. We asked how far to the next town. "Town?" he said; "Which way did you come?" We told him. "Why, you left the nearest town sixty-five miles back," he said. "Nothing in this other direction till you get to Chinle, and that's not hardly a town, just a school and hospital and a couple of trading posts." We asked him if he didn't get lonely. "Well, no," he said, "I don't have much chance to get lonely. Too many Indians around for that. Guess you saw all those huts they call *hogans* as you came up the road?" We told him we didn't see a house till we got to his. "Well, they aren't exactly houses, not like this one at any rate. But there's plenty of them. You must have passed fifteen from the time you left the highway. They're in plain sight of the road, too."

"What kind of Indians live out here?" we asked. "Navahos, all Navahos, finest kind of people you'd want to deal with," the trader replied.

"Isn't it rather dangerous for you to be here all alone, one white man to so many Indians?" This threw the trader into a fit of laughing that lasted till a dark-skinned man, in a blue shirt and pants and a big hat, came in the door. The trader stopped long enough to say something to him in a strange language, and then they both laughed. When the trader could speak once more he said, "I guess you are pretty new in this country, aren't you?" We admitted it was our first trip. "Well, I'll tell you, strangers, you're safer out here going to sleep beside the road with fifty dollars on your chest than you are in New York City with fifty cents in your pocket and your eyes wide open. We're civilized folks out here. May not have all the modern conveniences, but at least we know enough to behave ourselves. Isn't that right, *Hosteen?*" The Indian nodded. "He can understand English but he doesn't like to speak it," the trader explained. "He's one of about a dozen educated ones around here that can't do anything with English. They went to school for a while, but seems like they didn't learn much English."

We took our leave and drove back the way we had come. Sure enough, here and there half a mile or so off the road we could see rounded humps of earth, made more conspicuous now by the thin blue smoke rising from the top of the dome. In a few places we saw flocks of sheep coming home in the evening, and once a little boy peered at us from behind a bush.

This happened a number of years ago. Since then we have lived with the Navahos in their round, earth-covered hogans, we have travelled with them, and read about them. We have visited their schools and hospitals, and have talked with the people who teach them and care for their sick and administer their affairs.

Our purpose was simply to try to understand the Navahos' way of looking at things, and to compare their point of view with our own and that of people brought up like ourselves in average American communities. Soon, as we observed and learned and some of our preconceived notions began to dissolve, we became fascinated with the problem of the mutual adjustment and cooperation between people who are separated by language, skin color, and a whole way of life. Inherent in this adjustment, it seemed to us, were some of the keys to the strife and wars of all the world.

It was obvious that we could not study all the world, but we could study the Navahos. Out of this particular case, we thought, we might learn a few principles of more general value. Being physicians, we were naturally interested in the specific question of health, and we devoted a large amount of our attention to ways in which greater freedom from sickness might be brought to the Navahos, and Indian and white man's ideas on the subject might be mutually adjusted.

THE NAVAHO DOOR

Invent some manner of realizing your own ideals which will also satisfy the alien demands—that and that only is the path of peace.

William James

LOOKING BACKWARD

BEFORE COLUMBUS CAME, the continents of North and South America were populated by Indian people who shared a yellow-brown skin and black straight hair, but who had little else in common. They were more remarkable for diversity of type than for similarity. In North America there are about twenty-eight Indian language stocks, fewer in Central America and more in South America; most of these stocks include many languages and within some languages many dialects. Conditions of living and culture varied as widely as did language. The wildest men lived at the extreme north and the extreme south of the continents, while the central part was the home of the most highly evolved society. It was similar to the situation in the eastern hemisphere, where the Mediterranean basin nurtured the highest ancient European culture between black savages in the south and white savages in the north.

In the northwestern woods of what is now Canada and Alaska lived Athabascan-speaking people who hunted with bow and arrow and with pit and dead-fall traps. They ate some wild fruits but caribou meat was the staple of their diet; they lived in drafty bark huts, and wore skin clothing, had no pottery and little art. Tribal organization was slight. Independent families roamed the forest

3

and were familiar with famine and freezing. They lived and died in the wilderness with as little impression on surrounding life as mice in a meadow.

At the tip of South America lived people (the Alacaluf, the Yahgan, and the Ona) similar to the Athabascans of the north, but even ruder. In spite of a climate that was wet and cold all the time, they went naked, and their huts kept out neither the wind nor the rain. They could wander nude all day along the shore with the sleet blowing on them, then drop off to sleep in a dripping beech wood. They were probably physically the toughest people on earth. In crude canoes in which they built little fires they went fishing, and it was these little fires bobbing over the water at night that caused Magellan to name the coast behind them the Land of Fire, Tierra del Fuego.

Central America and northern South America were the regions of highest culture (that of the Mayans, the Aztecs, and others). Here existed complex, efficient, communal governments, which levied taxes, maintained armies, and established codes of law. The people cast and wrought gold and silver ornaments, and metal armor for their warriors, made mirrors of obsidian, and wove feather cloaks in mosaic pattern. In sea-going boats they traded as far as Cuba. They domesticated a great number of the still-valuable food plants. They invented writing and created parchment to record it and they had a literature and an educational system, with different schools for boys and girls. They understood a great deal about the movements of the heavenly bodies, made a calendar that showed a knowledge of the exact length of the year, and invented the mathematical concept of zero. Their architecture was massive and elaborate. Religion permeated all of life, and was often gory and gruesome, with emphasis on sacrifice.

In part of what is now New Mexico and Arizona were the villages and farms of the Pueblo Indians—the outposts of civilization. They lived by hunting, raising corn, squash and beans, and by gathering wild fruits; they understood irrigation, and ground their corn between stones to make flour. Dogs and turkeys were domesticated and cotton was cultivated to supply material for weaving cloth. Some of the buildings were made of earth and wood, but these Indians also understood building in stone, and many of their structures are still standing. Pottery making was highly developed.

The Pueblo Indians had art in most things and religion in everything. Life was a complicated changing series of ritual patterns whose order and place were dictated by tradition and by the priests. Most of the ritual was directed at bringing rain, on which life depended in a semi-arid region, but part was also directed against sickness. Their culture held in check aggression and strong emotions; they cultivated harmony and an even trend of living.

It is not known exactly how or when the Navahos came, but the evidence from linguistics, archaeology and tradition suggests that about 1300 A.D., or possibly as much as two to three hundred years earlier, bands of the Athabascans, the woodland hunters of the north, came roving down the mountain chains and desert valleys into the land of the Pueblos. They came like the Goths and Vandals on rural Italy, moving into the unoccupied canyons. They lived by hunting, by gathering wild vegetable food, and by robbing the Pueblos. It may have been for this reason that many of the Pueblos began living in fortified towns and high on mesas that could be defended, such as Oraibi and Acoma, and from which they have only recently begun to descend.

The contacts were not all warlike. These Athabascans learned farming, weaving, and how to live in an all-pervasive, mystic religion, from the Pueblos, but greatly changed all three in terms of their own traditions and feelings.

One afternoon in 1492, while exploring the West Indian Islands, Columbus had some natives aboard and tried to learn a little of their language. He made notes on five words, probably the very first recording of an Indiàn tongue: *strong man, gold, heaven, home, nothing*. The forgotten native who gave these words all unconsciously outlined the succeeding four hundred years of his race. *Strong men* from Europe came after *gold,* breaking up the native culture and preaching their ideas of *heaven* at the sword's point, built their *homes* everywhere and pushed the natives closer and closer to *nothing*. The first to fall were the Aztecs in 1519, and the last were the Yaquis in 1886.

About 1540 the Spanish came pushing up from Central America and conquered the Pueblos, but not the Athabascans. These Indians fought both the Pueblos and the Spanish and grew rich through plunder. They took sheep, horses and cattle from the Spanish, and obtained many new recruits to their tribe by the adoption of prisoners and refugees from other Indian groups. Consequently, there was a corresponding acquisition of cultural traits and patterns.

Most likely the name *Navaho* arose at this time from the people of the Jemez pueblo who used to refer to one group of the Athabascans by a word that meant "farmer" and which the Spanish corrupted to "Navajo." But even now the Navahos do not use that name when talking to each other; they say "Dineh," which means "The People."

In the seventeenth and eighteenth centuries, after the Spanish had the Pueblos in what is now New Mexico completely subdued, they began to press the Navahos harder, but they never felt strong enough to attempt to round them up. Many Navahos retreated into the deep, winding Canyon de Chelly, where they raised their crops and from which they raided on horseback the Spanish and the other Indians.

In 1848 the United States acquired New Mexico and Arizona from Mexico and attempted to come to terms with the Navahos, but there were numerous broken treaties on both sides. With the Navahos this was largely because the loose tribal organization of their ancestors persisted, and what one chief promised did not bind other bands. As more and more settlers and cattlemen came to the west, they pushed deeply into the Navaho country, and the Indians were soon fighting for their lives and living-space. The Americans sent their army, organized the Mexicans and hired the Utes and other tribes, until all hands were against the Navahos. They were killed at sight, and if they escaped, their crops and sheep were destroyed, leaving them without food.

There are numerous stories of Navaho life when it was at its most hazardous stage. One old man said his parents told him: "The children would eat wild potatoes without even cleaning them off, and the older people just tightened up the broad belts they wore so they wouldn't feel hungry. The Utes would come to a home and kill most of the people, maybe two or three would escape. Those that got away might not have any food or shoes or even clothes."

Another said: "My father told me about Zunis, Mexicans, Lagunas and some white men. 'That is why you have to get up early in the morning, roll in the snow and get your body hard and strong. Roll in water. If you do that way, never get scared of any one. If you don't do that, somebody is going to beat you up right now. These people had guns and knives, so they might kill you. You can't beat him, but have to fight a little. Might kill him some way.' My father said, 'Better get good guns and powder in a sack, then enemies be afraid. If some time at midnight when you are asleep a bunch of people come and are going to get you, if you have got good guns, you can jump out of bed and try to fight them, and if you have worked hard, then you can scare them.' "

Still another: "My people told me I was born when my mother was running away from the Mexicans. When the bad pain start she was alone, so she reached up and caught the branch of a pine tree, and held on to that and I was born and fell right down on the ground, down on the pine needles, and rolled a little way down the hill. My mother wrapped me in a bit of rag and got down in a ditch with me and hid."

These dreadful days reached their peak in 1863 when Colonel Kit Carson brought an army to Canyon de Chelly and made prisoners of 9000 of a possible 14,000 to 15,000 Navahos. They were marched three hundred miles eastward to a concentration camp at Fort Sumner. Today Navahos refer to this event as "The Long Walk." While in this captivity they practiced the silversmithing for which they have become famous. It had come from the Mexicans but, as with weaving, the Navahos developed it highly along their own lines.

At the end of five years they were allowed to go back to their own regions. They made a promise to keep peace, and they have kept their promise. It is said that their leaders tied a goat to a tree and, while it butted itself fruitlessly against the trunk, the tribe filed by and took it as an object-lesson on the uselessness of resisting the United States Government.

A reservation was set aside for the Navahos, one much smaller than the territory they now inhabit, and the administration of the agency was centered at Fort Defiance. The Government gave them a few sheep and some clothing and farm implements; in time, boarding schools were built for the children.

The Navahos, however, found themselves beset with difficulties. They had to live in a land where earning a living was not easy and, in spite of being on a reservation, they were constantly subjected to pressure from white people. This was a period of great self-satisfaction on the part of Americans, and it didn't occur to anyone that there could be the slightest virtue in the way the Indians had been living for centuries. Indeed, many white people thoroughly mistrusted the Indians and felt that the ordinary laws of fair dealing did not apply to them. As a result the Indians were exploited, tricked and robbed, and in many of the disputes between Indian and white the Government was very slow to come to the Indian's aid, largely because of fear of political pressure.

As a reaction to the uncertainties of life and a well-founded fear and mistrust of their powerful conquerors, the Navahos drew a circle around themselves, shutting out all others and strengthening their own culture, but at the same time they made an economic adjustment to the whites by developing flocks of sheep and making blankets and silver for sale.

Today, in spite of having been crushed in war, in spite of living in a semi-arid country where getting a living is difficult, in spite of having been persecuted and exploited, the Navahos emerge with their numbers increased from 14,000 or 15,000 at the time of the captivity to over 50,000, with their own culture functioning, and yet adjusted to the economic demands of the surrounding white civilization.

This does not mean that they have settled the problems of their existence. At this moment they are in as precarious a position as they have ever been because of their large numbers; their big flocks overgrazing the land; the progression of an erosion cycle in the Southwest; the advent of keen economic competition with whites and with each other; and the ever-present threat of political pressures which again permit the Indians to be victimized by private interests.

As one looks backward at the road whites and Indians have travelled together, and at their relationships today, one cannot help wondering if America is really prepared to lead the world in race tolerance and international peace. Certainly, as a nation, we have had the experience, but have we built on it towards something better? It is vastly easier to be informed and to take the right action in connection with people who are within our boundaries than it is to do so across oceans and in foreign lands, even with the modern speed of travel and reporting. Therefore, if we do not live up to our avowed principles in dealing with those near at hand, what chance is there of success in distant parts?

In modern times it is rare that as a nation we have displayed conscious rapacity towards the Navahos or other Indians, but we have a way of inventing excuses for taking from the Indian what we want, whether it is cheap labor or land. We are then in the comfortable position of having the material advantage we desire and at the same time feeling virtuous. One of our most common excuses is that the Indian has certain faults which are "racially characteristic." He is "unable to farm his land properly," therefore we must take it from him for the good of the nation. He is "incapable of a higher standard of living," hence it only ruins him to give him more wages, and so on. Anthropology has never found any evidence to confirm these assumptions, but our rationalization is human and comfortable, and the ideas live on.

While looking out across the world in which we wish to establish a lasting peace when the war is over, we must consider the future. Our capacity for rationalization in dealing with the Indians has contributed to their demoralization, but because the Indians are few and weak, we have been harmed relatively little in any physical sense. When it comes to dealing with other nations and other races around the earth, the matter will be different. As victors in the war, we shall be strong, but not strong enough to bend the entire world to our profit.

It is hardly possible to maintain one standard of international and inter-racial relationships outside the country and another for the Indians and other minorities within the United States. It is to be hoped that through our experience we may build constructively across cultural lines both inside and outside the nation.

ENVIRONMENT AND SOCIETY

THERE ARE ABOUT 370,000 Indians in the United States today. Of this number, approximately one-half are of full blood, and one-half mixed, chiefly with whites, though a few groups are mixed with negroes. There are about two hundred different tribes, and they speak about as many different languages. These tribes cannot understand each other unless they speak English or Spanish or use the sign-language. At least 50,000 Indians know only their native tongue.

Map I gives an idea of the diversity of Indian cultures within the United States with which the Indian Office has to deal, and it also indicates the relationship of the Navahos to the rest of the Indian scene.

Map II shows the actual reservations and settlements, and it can be seen that the Navaho Reservation is by far the largest. This reservation is partly in four states, New Mexico, Arizona, Colorado and Utah, but the greatest portion is in Arizona. The area is about sixteen million acres, or twenty-five thousand square miles, which is approximately the size of New Hampshire, Vermont, and Rhode Island put together. Besides the Navahos on the reservation, there are many living on about two million acres adjoining it. The entire region is a rocky plateau, averaging six thousand feet elevation, rising higher

in mountains, which is cut deeply by canyons and washes. At present
it is very dry, and the chief cover is sagebrush, pinyon, and cedar,
with large pines and poplars in the mountains, and cottonwoods in
the canyons.

Within the memory of living Navahos, the country was remarkably different. A man about fifty years old said, "Back in that time it
rained quite often, so people raised pretty good corn and squashes,
watermelon, muskmelon, what we don't plant now. Through that
rainy time the country was very good, the grass was growed so high
and everything looks good. Like that time, I remember, the sunflower was so high they was little over a pony."

One factor responsible for the change in the vegetation is the large
number of sheep and goats that have eaten and trampled the grass.
Another is that an erosion cycle began in 1880 and still continues,
and the little and big arroyos drain the water off so fast in some
places that it has no chance to soak into the ground. The figure
for the annual rainfall is between five and ten inches, thirty-seven
per cent of which, fortunately, falls during the growing season in
July and August. By way of comparison, the annual rainfall for
Maryland is forty-three inches. If the rain varies much in its distribution, that is, if it falls too soon or too late or too scantily while the
plants are growing, the crops fail entirely. Then, again, the entire
rainfall for the month may come in one shower, and often the storms
are so violent that crops are destroyed by them. The summer of 1939
was extremely dry and only a few of about one hundred families in
an area off the reservation which we were studying succeeded in
bringing their corn to maturity. The others had all planted and
cultivated their fields, but the corn had shriveled up in spite of their
best efforts.

The temperature varies from 98° or more above zero to 24° below.
Although in winter it is usually mild during the day if the sun
shines, it is often below freezing after sundown. In summer the sun
is hot, but it is pleasantly cool in the shade and at night. The wind
blows frequently, swirling the dust and driving it into everything.
Violent changes of weather come suddenly; in 1931 four feet of snow
fell in a single night. Late and early frosts are a further hazard to

agriculture, and since the growing season averages only about ninety-eight days and corn requires ninety to one hundred and forty days to mature, there is little margin for variation. It is probable that living in a world where the results of half a year's work can be wiped out in a few days or a few hours has contributed to the Navahos' tendency to rely on mystic religion rather than on material things. The comforts that come from mystic belief are more reliable than the comforts of crops, stock, and household possessions. It is possible also that the Navaho's experience with life's uncertainties makes him profoundly mistrust the future and consequently tend to spend what he has rather than save it. Such feelings may underlie what at first sight we are likely to call "shiftlessness."

In some areas on the reservation there is no wood for many miles, but in other regions it is plentiful, particularly pinyon and cedar. Wood is needed for fuel and house building. The Navahos prefer dry dead wood for burning which is often hauled for several miles; but they cut living trees for making houses.

The water supply comes from melted snow in winter, and from springs, dams and artesian wells in summer. As one might suspect, the Navahos spend many hours in taking their barrels miles to water sources every few days. The quality of the water varies greatly, and in some places it is so alkaline or so muddy that it is scarcely fit to drink.

In spite of these practical disadvantages, the country is beautiful, full of magnificent mountains and valleys, brilliant skies, gaudy sandstone cliffs and buttes, park-like stretches of huge pine trees or small pinyon and cedar, fields of wild flowers in spring and summer, and nearly everywhere the soft grayish-green of sage.

It is a tribute to the Navahos' hardiness and persistence that they have managed not only to exist but also to increase almost four-fold in seventy years. It would be easy to believe that a dense population could not cope with the scarcity of food resources and water in this area, and perhaps partly for that reason the Navahos live in widely separated family groups. The family's neighbors are as far as a mile away, unless they are close relatives, and often the next group will be five or six miles distant. Except for a few sections, near the mountains or the rivers, such as Tohatchi and Shiprock, most of the farming is carried on without irrigation and is dependent on rainfall. Old-fashioned native methods of preparing the ground for seed have given way to plowing with iron plows and cultivating with iron hoes. Families who do not own these implements themselves, can usually borrow them from a neighbor.

The principal crops raised are corn of many colors, squash, beans and melons. The thinnings and flowers of these crops are eaten as well as the fruit, in all stages of maturity, and this is, of course, a good economic adjustment. In a few areas alfalfa and wheat are grown. The farmers have various ways of drying and storing their harvest for use through the winter. These crops, and meat from their sheep and goats, form the chief diet of the Indians, although nowadays many products of our civilization are also used whenever they can be obtained, such as, coffee, sugar, wheat flour, baking powder, salt, dried fruit, rice, and whatever else the Navaho can afford. The mutton they use is generally very tough and has a strong taste, but it is greatly relished, especially the fat. One Indian said, "It seems like you are getting more when it's tough." They gather a certain number of wild fruits, such as the yucca and the prickly pear cactus. It is advantageous for them to stick as close to their native diet as is compatible with health, for in so doing they reduce the degree of their dependence on money, and little money is available to the average Navaho. The more they produce for themselves, the farther the cash they earn goes in securing things they need. In recent years many efforts have been made by the Government to improve the Indian's agricultural success. Stockmen are sent to give advice, and pupils in the high schools are taught modern methods of agriculture.

When one considers their recent history and the vicissitudes of their daily life, it is little wonder that the Navahos are a conservative people; but they are changing, as any old-timer can tell you. Before they will accept new methods, however, it has to be proved to them that they will receive some advantages from them.

The climate makes a certain amount of shelter necessary, against cold in winter and the hot sun in the summer. For the cold, a log

Mesa Verde National Park photograph

A Mesa Verde National Park Diorama Showing Famous Cliff Palace

Homes of People Who Lived in These Canyons before the Navahos Came

and mud house, called a *hogan* and shaped somewhat like a beehive, with a central fire, keeps the family comfortable. Formerly, this fire simply burned on the dirt floor in the center of the hogan, the smoke finding its way to the smoke hole above not too effectively, but in recent years the Navahos have constructed stoves and flues out of old oil drums and tin cans, so that the smoke finds its way to the vent more directly. The house fire is kept going all night during the cold weather because most families do not have enough blankets to keep them warm. In summer they move to a brush windbreak to get the benefit of the cool night air, and during the day they keep the sun off by shades made of old boxes, boards, and brush, known as "squaw coolers."

The men wear blue denim pants and gay shirts, and the women bright colored full-flounced skirts made of sateen or calico and velveteen blouses decorated with silver buttons. In winter they add extra layers of these same clothes, and use blankets and sheepskin coats which they buy from the traders.

It is plain to see that many of their habits of living are affected by the demands of their environment. They must work hard just to keep alive. Much time has to be spent in getting water, and the water must be used sparingly. They have to keep a supply of fire wood on hand, plant and cultivate their crops diligently, harvest before frost strikes, and they must care for their sheep and goats. The whole family takes part in these pursuits, usually the men or big boys do the heavy work, and the women look after the house, the cooking, weaving, making of clothes and taking care of the children. Most of the women are able to do the heavy work if there is no man around, and most men have learned to cook when they are out herding away from home. In general, the Navahos are hard workers, but not systematic.

Considering how little water there is, it is surprising how much cleaning is done. Faces are washed every morning, and hands several times a day. Every little while there is a wash-day for clothes. The dishes are generally rinsed off between meals. Some Navahos have said that the appearance of these habits is one of the principal evidences of school training among their people.

The difficulties of such physical surroundings are reflected in the health of the people. Doctors working on the reservation are always impressed by the small number of really robust children. Those who come to school are usually in much better condition after they have been there a little while than those who remain at home. These children are mostly undernourished, and have chronic colds, until they achieve their full growth. Tuberculosis is common among both adults and children. There is little understanding of the contagiousness of this disease, and great reluctance to take the sick person to the sanitarium until he is about to die. In spite of the sunshine and fresh air, the closeness of contact in the often over-crowded hogans and the freedom with which the people spit makes the spread of infection pretty common. Another scourge was trachoma, but since the coming of sulfanilamide it is rapidly being eradicated. (Sulfanilamide was discovered to be a very effective treatment of trachoma by the Indian Service doctors.)

To give you a little more definite idea of how these people live, let us follow one family through a winter's day. This family includes a husband and wife, two grown children by a former marriage, six children by his present wife, ranging from ten years to one month, and an old man of about seventy-five married to the grown daughter. This is an unusually large family, because the death rate among Navaho children is high.

There is a general stirring that begins as soon as the first light shows in the east. They start to get up, build the fire, wash their faces, and cook breakfast. Those still sleeping are waked at sunup. Wood is chopped, horses located and brought near the house, snow gathered in pans and put to melt, and if the sheep are being herded near home, they are taken out of the corral to graze. Breakfast consists of a large flat baking powder biscuit, called "Indian bread," cooked on a griddle, coffee and perhaps meat. Sometimes they boil corn-meal mush, rice, or cereal for the children. The men eat first, and then the women and children. After breakfast the men go out about their business, and the women pick up the sheepskins and blankets that had been used during the night and either hang them out to air or on racks in the house, to get them out of the way. The accumulated ashes are shoveled from the fireplace and carried outside, and the house is swept with a branch of sagebrush. The children are tidied, their faces washed, their hair brushed and tied back. When the house is warm enough the baby has her bath in a basin near the fire, and afterward is fed and put to sleep. Then the women start the work of the moment. For many weeks this consists in sorting beans that are to be used as seeds.

The old man meanwhile rides off on his horse to the trader's or to see one of his cronies. The father and the grown son help with getting wood or water, or hire out to work. When the sun gets to the position that they judge to indicate noon, the women, children, and anyone else who is around have a meal which is the same as breakfast. The men present are likely to sit around and smoke and talk for a while after eating, while the women listen and wash the dishes. For the afternoon the activities are much the same as in the morning. Sometimes the ten-year-old girl spends several hours carding wool while her mother spins it into thread and her half-sister dyes it in a kettle on the fire. When there is enough spun and dyed wool on hand, the loom is set up and a rug woven, which is an important source of the family's cash income.

Toward sundown the family gathers again and supper is prepared, similar to the other meals, but always including meat if it is available. After eating they talk and tell stories, lying on sheepskins with their feet toward the fire, or sitting propped against a saddle, the fire casting a flickering light on their brown faces and filling the air with the fragrant smell of cedar. The children sit quietly or play with each other until they get drowsy, and then wrap themselves in blankets and lie down to sleep. They sleep very soundly, even in the midst of a good deal of commotion. Unless something special is going on, the rest of the family goes to sleep at nine or ten o'clock, but if company is present they often talk and smoke until midnight or after.

Considering the physical environment, and attendant difficulties, the Navahos have a hard time earning a living. In fact, by our standards they do not earn a living, for their wages and financial resources do not approach what we would consider a minimum subsistence. In 1940 the average Navaho's income was $82.00, of which $36.00

came from livestock, $24.00 from wages, $12.00 from agriculture, $7.00 from rugs, and $3.00 from miscellaneous sources. Since the average Navaho family consists of about seven members, this makes the family income for a year $574.00, which includes the estimated value of crops and stock used for food as well as actual cash. Since the war started, many Navahos have held defense jobs and cash income has increased considerably.

There are a number of sources of income. Families who own sheep sell their wool in the spring and their lambs in the fall; those who have good farming land and raise more produce than they need for themselves sell it. When, every few years, large crops of wild pinyon nuts appear on the trees, whole families of Navahos go off and camp where they are plentiful, to gather the nuts for sale to the traders. They enjoy the outing as well as the income. Although a large percentage of the women weave rugs, if they have to pay for their wool this is not a very profitable occupation. In fact, one trader, by hiring an expert weaver, found that at the current market value of the rug, this woman could expect to receive only five cents an hour for her time. A number of the men make beautiful silver jewelry. The Indians work for each other to some extent, herding and farming, and they also hire out to white traders and ranchers. A good many had jobs with the Government under the CCC or now have positions in the Indian Service. The medicine men, although they do not work steadily by any means, get rather good fees.

A few Navahos who have exceptionally good farming and grazing land have considerable fortunes. Like ourselves, these Indians regard highly the possession of money and goods, but any person who by chance or industry becomes wealthy is expected to share this wealth with less fortunate relatives and friends. They have a feeling that a very wealthy man probably got his money dishonorably, and they become sure of it if he does not distribute his surplus generously. With livelihood a hard problem for most people, a man with more than he needs is like one who ropes off a water hole in a dry country and will not let others drink. In their eyes he is mean and not acting like a Navaho. This social pattern, added to the mistrust of the future and belief in the present, which has been previously described in con-

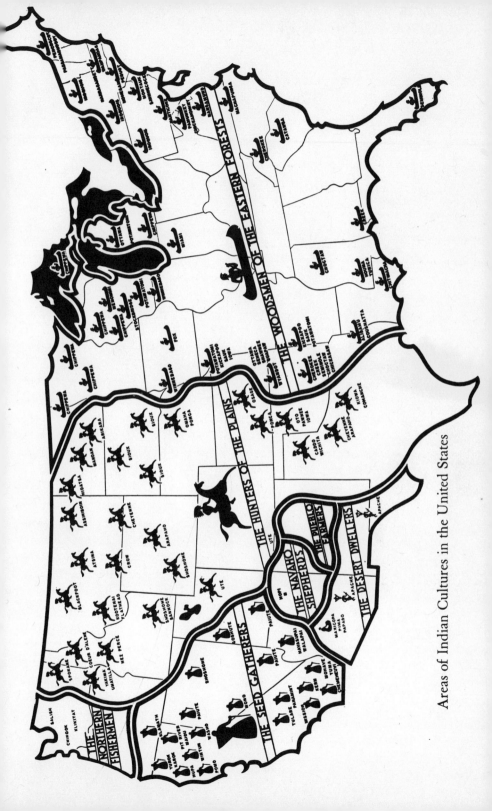

Areas of Indian Cultures in the United States

nection with their historical experiences and the forces of physical environment, further tends to make the Navaho a spendthrift. It is easy for white people who see successful Indians giving away their goods and money to consider them shiftless and extravagant. The Navaho, however, must follow this pattern of behavior if he does not wish his people to be against him.

Bank accounts as we know them are practically nonexistent among the Indians, for as soon as they get their money they spend it. A considerable amount goes for gambling, drinking, tobacco, and travelling around the country, but they do not spend all of it so recklessly. They buy clothes, jewelry, saddlery, religious objects, animals, farm machinery, and automobiles, and these investments often take the place of a bank. In time of need they can either be traded or be pawned with the trader as a bond for supplies received on credit. As a matter of fact, Navahos generally pawn much of their jewelry whenever they do not want to wear it, and let the trader keep it for safety.

The mother is the center of the family and the family home is most often near her maternal relatives. The husband and wife do not usually share the same house with the wife's parents because it is forbidden for a son-in-law to see his mother-in-law, but they live near-by, and the children and wife are in and out of her mother's house all the time. The children belong to the mother, and are members of her clan; in case of divorce they generally remain with her.

Property owning is strongly individual. Even the tiny children are given a few animals, and the older people take care of this stock until the children are able to do it themselves. The woman sells her own rugs, crops, and stock, and spends the money as she sees fit. The man does the same with his wages and the proceeds of his silversmithing, horse trading, farming, and stock raising. In general the women own most of the property, animals, and crops.

Ignorance of these customs can readily lead to misunderstanding the Indian. There is a story of an Indian approaching a trading post riding on a horse while his wife trudged behind on foot. The trader went up to the man and asked rebukingly, "Why is your wife walking?" The Navaho replied, "Because she ain't got a horse." To the trader this was an amusing example of Indian indifference, but in terms of Navaho custom it was a sensible reply. Since, as a woman, she probably owned most of the family property, it was her own lookout if she did not choose to convert some of it into a horse.

In former times when the man was active in hunting, raiding, and war parties, he was the dominant figure in the family. Now it is often the woman who controls the subsistence through her sheep and trading. The man still represents the family in public and at ceremonials, but the woman holds a good position and is respected and honored for her counsel as well as for her motherhood and earning capacity.

The children are one of the chief concerns of the adults and are cared for as well as the family's means and knowledge permit. Both parents, of course, invest much of their earnings in food and clothes for the family. Naturally, there are exceptions to this in people who do not like children, who are lazy and indifferent, or who exploit the children for their work.

There are some advantages in the usual Navaho method of training. The baby of the family is spoiled by everyone until the next child arrives, but then it takes a more grown-up place in the group and receives much less attention. As soon as a child is able to walk around, it begins to have a small share in the family's work and mutual living, first walking to the wood pile with its elders, then bringing in chips, helping to put the dishes away, running errands, and gradually as it grows older taking a more active and responsible part in family life. Much of the children's play consists in imitating the work activities of the grown-ups. Ideals of industry are constantly held up to the children, and they are encouraged in learning the techniques of weaving, farming, herding, stock management, wood cutting, and building, when they show any interest in them. At the same time there is little pressure put on the children to do work for which they have no liking.

The family is a closely knit and interdependent unit, each member of which contributes a certain amount to the up-keep of the whole, either in work or supplies. The division of labor and co-operation within the family makes life easier and pleasanter for all its members, and is almost a necessity under the environmental and economic conditions of their life. The unfortunate side of this arrangement is that the compliant and dependent children may be worked very hard without receiving adequate compensation, either in clothes or stock, an exploitation which they later resent bitterly and which may make them suspicious of other Navahos. This matter of exploiting the children has been noticed by the teachers, who find that sometimes the most hard-working and dependable child is kept home and the less able ones are sent to school. No doubt in some cases this indicates laziness and neglect on the part of the parents, but often it is a necessity.

There are three forms of marriage practised by the Navahos. One is according to white custom in which all the civil laws regulating marriage and divorce must be observed; another is the elaborate native "basket ceremonial," with exchange of gifts, which corresponds somewhat to our church wedding. The third and probably the commonest form is also native and resembles our common law marriage. In this form there is no ceremonial, but the families and relatives concerned are agreed about the match and give the couple some assistance in building a hogan and setting up a household near the girl's mother.

A good many Navahos have more than one wife, usually two. Sometimes this turns out well for all concerned, with the two wives sharing the work of the household between them, but at other times there is bickering and fighting. It is hard for many white people to look on such a custom without disgust, and at one time the Government tried to end it by decree. To families of many years' standing this was a drastic measure amounting almost to a death warrant for those to be cast out. A number of cases of men killing their wives and themselves caused the Government to stop this effort.

Faithfulness in married couples is not considered to be as important as we consider it, but is believed to be the personal concern of the individual partners. The Navahos, however, are not immune to jealousy, and if there is too much promiscuity, there is likely to be resentment, quarreling and separation. It is not considered much of a disgrace to have a child without being married, and children born out of wedlock are treated the same as any others.

While the core of the family, that is, the mother and her children, is stable, the male side may shift without causing any great upheaval. In the marriages by Navaho custom, divorce is simply a matter of one or both parties deciding to separate, in which case the man returns to his family. There is often bitterness and unhappiness over separation, but on the whole the Navahos take the making and breaking of marriage much more as a matter of course and much less sentimentally than we.

A Navaho feels himself a part not only of his immediate biological family, but also of what has been called his "extended" family. This consists of his mother's family and his father's family, reaching far beyond the easily recognized degrees of relationship to those whose ancestors were near relatives of his own ancestors, and shades off into the clan. When two Navahos meet, one of the first questions asked is, "To what clan do you belong?" The answer indicates the maternal line. Directly following this question, "For what clan were you born?" is asked—meaning "What is your father's line?" These two questions show that although clan membership and inheritance of property is through the mother, the descent from and relationship to the father's line is also of importance. If a family is broken up and the children are not kept by the mother and her parents for some reason, it is quite frequently found that they become the responsibility of the father's parents.

The clan is a unit of considerable social importance. There are certain things that clan members expect to do for and receive from other members of the clan. At one time the clans were grouped into bands that were led by chiefs, but there are no chiefs of importance today. One aspect of clans that often causes trouble for whites working with the Navahos is that they give rise to many more terms for kinship relationships than can be expressed simply in the English language. When speaking English, Navahos often use terms like "mother," "father," "sister," and "cousin" in ways that are confusing to white people. For instance, "father" may mean the real biological father, but it may also mean any man of the father's generation in his clan. Similarly, "mother" may be used for the real mother, her sisters or the father's sisters, women members of the clan of the mother's generation, or perhaps a foster mother who may not be related in any way. The same thing might be said for "brother," "sister," or "cousin." Thus, if you are trying to discover family relationships and ask a boy if another boy is his brother, he may say yes. You cannot rest with this but must find out if he means real brother, that is, if they had the same mother and father, or just what relatives they do have in common. Most likely you will find that they have no relatives in common, but that they merely belong to the same clan. Probably unless the Indian speaks very good English, you never will unravel the relationship.

For the sake of the records and one's own sense of understanding, it would be worth while for the doctor, nurse, teacher, or other person working among the Navahos, to try to learn a few of the kinship terms in the Navaho language. Some of them are sufficiently specific so that they indicate at once the relationship between two people. These terms are listed at the end of this book.

RELIGION

RELIGION ENTERS every phase of Navaho life. It is scarcely ever out of their minds from the time they are old enough to understand anything about it. Every Navaho man and woman knows and performs some rituals, prayers, songs, and legends. All through life each may collect new items and add to his store. These personal rites are used in planting, trading, house-building, care of stock, treating illness, warding off danger, and for general good hope; nearly all are expected to work by creating or maintaining harmonious living of man with the forces of the universe. Some of this lore is common knowledge, but much of it is secret. One person learns a bit from another and after he can perform it perfectly he pays for it to make it his own. Navahos buy songs and prayers from each other as they do jewelry.

The over-all emphasis in Navaho religion is on curing sickness, just as with the Zuni Indians it is on the production of rain. All religions are fundamentally systems for obtaining a sense of security. The Navahos stress the insecurity of illness, but their concept of disease is so broad that it reaches far beyond ours.

There are a very large number of causes of disease. At least thirty-two animals are supposed to bring illness, and of these the commonest are the bear, deer, coyote, porcupine, snake, and eagle. Ordinarily, contact with these animals does not bring misfortune, but under special circumstances, one may get sick from hunting the animal, being attacked by it, eating it, seeing it, and particularly dreaming about it. Dreams are always taken seriously as evidence of coming disaster. Lightning, wind, and to a certain extent the earth itself, may cause illness. A man may receive harm from lightning or a whirlwind, not only by being directly hit, but by being near where it has struck, or having anything to do with the objects struck. Any ceremonial may infect a person if he behaves improperly towards or during the ceremonial. Unborn children are thought to be particularly susceptible to disease and may catch the illness if either the father or the mother attends the ceremonial, even though no improper behavior occurs. The child may not immediately get sick; in fact, he may be an old man before the symptoms appear. Spirits of the dead are especially dangerous. Navahos are famous for their horror of corpses or anything that has touched a corpse. Night and darkness are dreaded because then the spirits are thought to be about. Casual contact with other tribes of Indians, Mexicans and whites, is considered a likely source of illness.

Witchcraft is considered an important source of sickness. Men or women, particularly the old and white-haired, and also the very poor or the very rich, may exert this malignant force. As with other cultures, the witches run counter to all the religious and moral laws. They murder their nearest and dearest friends and relatives, practice incest, handle corpses freely, robbing them of their burial jewels and using parts of their bodies for their incantations. They deliberately cause illness in others, sometimes merely from jealousy, sometimes so the victim will pay heavily to regain his health. The witch can work this without exposing himself by being a practising medicine man, and to all outward appearances produces his cures by regular ceremonial methods, whereas in reality he is merely reversing his own witchcraft. Witches always keep their real nature a secret and often pose as pleasant and kindly people.

It can be seen that this institution of witchcraft is at least a potential source of social uneasiness and mutual suspiciousness. At times when the Navahos are suffering from particular stress, such as after the return from Fort Sumner seventy years ago, and at the start of the stock-reduction program recently, numerous accusations of witchcraft and the murder of witches appear.

The symptoms caused by these various agents are not consistent, and there is not much correlation between the nature of the symptoms and the supposed nature of the agents. They include aches and pains of all sorts, disturbing dreams, and feeling bad all over.

There are thirty-five principal Navaho ceremonials, each with numerous possible variations. The majority are concerned with disease, but directed at treating what the Navahos consider first causes, which we have already mentioned, rather than at the symptoms. A curing ceremonial is given for one or more specific patients but the good effects of it are not limited to them. They extend to all who are present, particularly the family of the patient and those who live in the neighborhood. This influence helps the ailing and perpetuates health in the strong.

Besides the curing ceremonials, which constitute most of the thirty-five major named chants, there are some others. One of these is the Blessing Way, "A rite whose legends, songs and prayers are chiefly concerned with the creation and placement of the earth and sky, sun and moon, sacred mountains and vegetation, the inner forms of these natural phenomena, the control of the he and she rains, dark clouds and mist, the inner forms of the cardinal points and life phenomena that may be considered the harbingers of blessing and happiness." * This ceremonial is employed as a general means to ensure or restore harmony when it has been disturbed. Evil consists of discord between the forces of nature, and the Blessing Way is a means of recreating the harmony or of strengthening it. It is performed for girls at puberty, for pregnant women, for a returned traveler who has lived for a long time with non-Navahos, for a family after a death has occurred, for men going off to the army, and in general when the need is felt for "good hope." There are special

* Father Berard Haile: Some Cultural Aspects of the Navaho Hogan. Fort Wingate, Arizona, 1935.

ceremonials for hunting, for war, for trading, and for gathering salt, which were important in days past.

These various ceremonials are carried on by medicine men, whose Navaho titles are best put into English by the words Singer and Curer. They practice and direct the ceremonials which are believed to have been handed down in an unbroken chain, like the apostolic succession, from the time when the gods gave ceremonial power to the first Navahos.

The selection of a ceremonial is not the responsibility of a Singer, but of the family who hires him, often on the recommendation of a native diagnostician. When the family has decided what they want, they employ a Singer and he carries out his work thoroughly and conscientiously.

Being a Singer is an exacting job. Ceremonials take from two to nine days to perform, and the amount of detailed and exact knowledge required is staggering. It is not often that any one Singer knows more than two or three complete ceremonials, though he may know parts of many others. He is a specialist in a particular part of the total religious lore of the culture. A man becomes a Singer by serving an apprenticeship with an established Singer. He must learn hundreds of songs, full of old words whose exact meaning he may not know, and he must learn them perfectly, not merely the words but the precise tone and way of singing them, and he must learn a great number of rules about sequence. He must know how to find and prepare the herbs concerned, how to make the ceremonial objects, how to make the sand paintings, how to direct the dancers, and all the acts and procedures of the ceremonial, not only for himself but also for the patient, the helpers, and the audience, who always participate to some extent. In addition, if he wishes to be a first-rate man in his profession, he should know in detail the long and involved legends which describe the origin of the ceremonials.

A Navaho described the learning process thus: "When a man wanted to be a Singer he should start in the summer and get a good crop of corn and harvest it and store it, and then about the time the first snow flies, build him up a good hogan, and then haul plenty of

wood there to do a long time, and have a woman there, his mother
or somebody, to cook for them, cook that corn and make bread. Then
he gets a Singer and has him there in the hogan and they work and
keep at it. If they get too tired, then they can take a sweat bath and
next day they feel good and can go on with it again. They stay at it
until the first thunder, and then quit. Next summer the learner does
the same thing again, and the next winter goes on with the learning.
Do that for maybe five years. By that time learn two or three ceremonials."

Singers receive, depending on the length of the ceremonial and
how closely they are related to the patient, from five to five hundred
dollars or the equivalent in goods. A survey in one area by Dr. Clyde
Kluckhohn showed that a Singer works an average of five days out
of fourteen, Curers much less. Besides knowing the ritual, many
Singers know a good deal of practical medicine, such as opening
abscesses and setting bones. It is possible that some of their herbs
have medicinal properties that are unknown to us, as few have ever
been gathered in sufficient quantities for pharmacological analysis.

Due to his position of prestige, his personality, and his proven capacity for sound judgment, the Singer is usually an informal leader,
and people with various problems come to ask his advice. His effec-
tiveness as a Singer, however, is not necessarily linked to his personality and character. He can be a scamp, but if he performs his rituals
with perfection and knows his lore thoroughly, he will be none the
less effective for the patient.

Curers differ from Singers in that they know only fragments of
ceremonials and are paid very much less for their services. Curers are
employed when Singers are not available, for minor illnesses and
apprehensions, and when the family is unable or unwilling to stand
the expense of a complete ceremonial.

There is still another type of religious practitioner among the
Navaho, whose job it is to decide the causative agents of illness, that
is to say, what error in the past has made the patient liable to his
present sickness, and what ceremonial he should have to straighten
things out. These men are the "diagnosticians" already referred to
and, unlike the Singer and the Curer, they do not learn their craft

by long hours of hard work, but have the spirit enter into them and are suddenly inspired. The most common means of diagnosis is known as "hand-trembling," though a number of other techniques are also employed occasionally. On being summoned to help a patient the diagnostician does not have to "mess around asking questions and guessing," as one of them described the white doctor's technique, but goes directly to work. He washes his hands and then sits cross-legged near the patient. He offers a prayer to the Gila Monster spirit, asking that he be allowed to discover the nature of the disease and its treatment. After the prayer a song is started, and the diagnostician sits with eyes shut, face averted, and one hand, sprinkled with corn pollen, extended before him. Soon the hand begins to shake. This motion is said to be out of the control of the man, starting and stopping by itself. As the shaking progresses the diagnostician thinks of various diseases. One finger of the hand often draws figures in the dirt and rubs them out again. After a while the hand will draw one, and instead of erasing will pat and point toward it, which indicates to the diagnostician that he is thinking of the right cause at the moment. He then goes on to think of possible ceremonials and Singers until the correct ones are picked out in a similar manner by the hand. When all the desired information has been gathered, the hand stops trembling and the diagnostician opens his eyes and tells what he has learned. The signs made on the floor are not letters but are parts of the religious symbols, such as sandpainting figures.

The fees for the diagnostician are much less than those for the Singer, usually two dollars or the equivalent, and probably right in proportion to the amount of work involved. Many women are diagnosticians but they rarely become Singers. Diagnosticians sometimes use their powers to locate lost property or lost animals.

Comparing the Singer and the diagnostician, it may be said that both are mystic, but one uses handed-down rituals which if properly performed are expected to work with the regularity of a chemical formula, while the other moves by a divine stroke. These two religious trends are often labeled "priestcraft" and "shamanism," respectively, and are found all over the world. They permeate our culture no less than that of the Indians, as can be seen by examining the Episcopal and Roman Catholic Churches, Hebrew Synagogues, or the Oxford Group, Holy Rollers, Dunkards, and many others that could be named.

Besides their personal religious practices, the lay Navahos, of course, are both audience and patients for the ceremonials. In one area records kept over a period of time by Dr. Kluckhohn showed that the men spent approximately one-fourth to one-third of their productive hours in religious activity, and women one-sixth to one-fifth. This does not mean that all this while they are sitting in the hogan while the chant goes on, but includes time used going to and from ceremonials, gathering medicinal herbs and other necessary apparatus, hauling wood and water, preparing food, and doing all the various things required for a ceremonial. On the average, twenty per cent of the family income is devoted to religion.

It is natural for white people to assume that the religious leaders of the Indians dominate their people, and doubtless they do in some ways, yet this fact is very easy to overestimate. None of the three types of medicine men who have been described force their services on the people, but wait until requested to help. It is the common belief that influences lay Navaho and Singer alike, and to suppose that the Singer is a wily charlatan is to overestimate his cunning and to do an injustice to his character.

It is not easy to say why the Indians believe as they do, but the more closely we look, the more it becomes evident that the things which men believe are related to their history and the lives they have to lead, and answer deep needs. Beliefs can and do become cumbersome, bringing their owners handicaps and inabilities to meet changing circumstances, but in helping people adjust themselves, one must be sure he is not attacking beliefs and practices vital to their welfare.

The thirty-five ceremonials and the personal lore that have been mentioned are not independent pieces of "superstition," but form a part of one enormous loosely integrated pattern, which is Navaho religion. This vast, spreading, interwoven mosaic of thought and belief has a complexity, an intellectual quality, and a mysticism that

A Navaho Family

Photograph by the authors

Photograph by the authors

The Common Type of Hogan in the Wooded Areas

Photograph by Helen M. Post

The Summer Brush-Hogan or "Shade"

Where Wood Is Scarce More Earth Is Used in Hogan-Making

Photograph by U. S. Indian Service

suggest an oriental religion. It is a bond that touches all Navahos, binding them together in spite of individualistic tendencies and marking them off as the chosen people, in an arid fruitless land, surrounded by their conquerors.

The Navahos believe that before the days of men, supernatural Beings lived on the earth and had adventures and coped with evil monsters. There were major Beings and minor Beings, many identified with various forces in nature, and each had his personality and characteristics. In the course of their adventures, such as ridding the country of the monsters, they developed methods for doing these things. The methods were in part practical, but they were also magical and were worked by means of songs and rituals. After a time the Beings decided to leave the earth and go to permanent homes in the East, South, West, North, Zenith and Nadir. Before going they had a great meeting, at which they created the Navahos and taught them all the methods that they had developed. By these methods the Navahos could protect themselves against disease, famine, and war, and they could build houses, get food, travel, marry, and trade. This meeting at which the Navahos were created and given the god-like powers to control the natural forces of wind, lightning, storm, and animals, and to keep all these in harmony with each other, was in itself a ceremonial of the Beings and became one for the Navahos. It is the "Blessing Way," which we have already mentioned, and occupies a key position in the theological scheme. After creating the Navahos and teaching them, the Beings moved off to their various abodes, saying they would watch over the doings of men but never return until the Navahos forgot the "Blessing Way" and the world came to an end.

In addition to being of great religious significance, these ceremonials are the chief social gatherings of the Navahos. The Indians come together for a common purpose, like people who go to church, but in addition they do not miss the opportunity to exchange news, or to engage in sports, dances, horse races, or various religious games, and undoubtedly they enjoy the drama that the performance provides.

In order to present a more vivid picture of what a ceremonial is like we shall describe parts of one. Imagine a Navaho hogan in a pinyon clearing. One of the family "feels bad all over," and arrangements have been made with a Singer. For days they have been anticipating, laying in stores of food, notifying friends, shaking out their best clothes, and retrieving their jewels from pawn at the trader's store. There is excitement in the air, and children scurry around with more than usual boisterousness. When the Singer is seen approaching, bouncing over the ruts in an old car driven by an assistant, outward calm at once comes over the family. They hardly look in his direction as he comes to a stop, but after a little they welcome him with quiet dignity and conduct him inside. There is little religious activity on this day of arrival. In the evening, an hour or two after supper, the Singer may offer a prayer. Turning to the East he will address one of the deities who lives there: "I and the sick man and all the rest of the people who are here with us and who will come to this ceremonial, we all thank you, and we are sure glad that you are with us and we are with you these nights and days. You should pray good for us. The songs should be the same way. You must give us good life, no sickness, for all these people that are here and also the neighbors out around, and also the white people. We must all get along. We should have good living, make a little money, have horses and sheep, what to live on. Especially give the young folks more lessons. Give us rain, we want the earth wet all the time so we can raise some crops. And about the feed, stock feed, grasses, give us that plenty, too." (As translated by a Navaho.)

The next morning at dawn the hogan is swept out, all the materials of daily life put away, and the fire removed from the center of the floor. The doorway is covered with blankets so no air can get in. The Singer and his helpers light a new fire using a fire drill, powdered lightning-struck rock, charcoal from the scar of a struck tree, while singing Lightning Songs. The patient and others who wish to join in the treatment undress outside. Four pokers are laid on the ground, radiating from the fire toward the cardinal points of the compass, the homes of the Beings. The pokers are made of carefully selected lightning-struck pinyon and cedar and represent men who chase evil away. The patient and the other participants enter the hogan and sit around the fire at specified spots. The heat is growing intense; the live coals represent lightning. The bull-roarer, which is a piece of wood from a lightning-struck tree carved in such a shape that it will whirl and make a roaring sound when swung on the end of a buckskin thong, and inlaid with turquoise and abalone shell to mark it with features, is taken outside by one of the Singer's helpers, made to roar, then brought in and applied to the patient. The sound is supposed to be thunder and the device was given to the Navahos by the Lightning Spirit. At the fire a pot is heating which contains an emetic composed of buckthorn, limberpine, bearberry, wild currant, juniper, and Colorado blue spruce. Each person gets a portion of it and washes himself all over beginning with the feet, then drinks and vomits. The Singer takes a brush made of wing and tail feathers from an eagle and an owl feather that fell out while the bird was flying, and brushes the patient, the others, and then the whole hogan, making motions that sweep evil toward the door. It is thought that evil is especially afraid of eagle feathers because one of the Beings adopted eagle children and brought them up to help the Navahos. The ends of the pokers are warmed and applied to the patient's body by the Singer. Then the others apply the pokers to themselves, rubbing the warm wood on any part that hurts. The patient and the other participants walk around the fire sunwise, stepping over the pokers. Evil cannot cross the pokers and thus they leave evil behind them. Then in succession, all jump over the fire, which represents lightning, again separating themselves from evil. Songs and prayers accompany each stage of the ritual. The heat is continuously very intense, and all sweat profusely. At the end of the ceremonial, the door blanket is lifted with one of the pokers, the bullroarer is made to thunder, and the patient steps out, followed by the others. After fire, ashes, and vomitus have been disposed of, all return and the Singer, using the eagle feathers, sprinkles the participants and the hogan with a fragrant lotion made of mint, horsemint, windodor and pennyroyal, kept in an abalone shell. Glowing coals are placed before each participant and on these is sprinkled a fumigant made of a plant root, sulphur, corn meal, and down from chickadee, titmouse, woodpecker, bluebird, and yellow warbler. These have been previously ground together by a virgin while the Singer sang special songs. Every one breathes the fumes and rubs them into his body. It is thought that they act as an anodyne. After this use, the coals are thrown out the smoke hole, taking evil with them.

This description passes over many details of importance, but even so, there is not space to give a similar account of all the details of the ceremonial. They include a ritual bath for the patient, sacrifices of turquoise and abalone, making sandpaintings, and many more things. With all the ritual performances, the Singer pours out songs that reflect their significance and divine origin.

On the last night of the ceremonial about two hours after supper, the final movement begins, and continues all night. The hogan is crowded with spectators, the firelight on their faces makes deep and moving shadows. The Singer and the patient sit on the west side facing east. All the women present sit on the north and men on the south. The Singer sings a verse of a song dealing with legends, things the Beings have done and the origin of the ceremonial, and the crowd takes it up with increasing volume. It is repeated and repeated that the patient is identified with the Beings. It is said that the Spirit of the Mountain belongs to the patient, his feet are the patient's feet, the patient walks in his tracks, and wears his moccasins. The Blue Horse spirit belongs to the patient, the turquoise horse with lightning feet, with a mane like distant rain, a black star for an eye and white shells for teeth, the horse spirit who feeds only on the pollen of flowers. There are songs that take up the patient's health directly, saying, "His feet restore for him, his mind restore for him, his voice restore for him." There are also repetitions of thoughts that proclaim all is well; thus, "My feet are getting better, my head is feeling better, I am better all over." Finally, it is said over and over again that all is being made beautiful and harmonious. The songs come in groups that form patterned relationships with each other. The effect of repetition, rhythm, and the antiphonal chorus is very impressive.

Before the first streak of dawn the Singer smears meal across the faces of the patient, himself and those who have performed well. This is to mark them out so the Beings will know them. When dawn begins, the patient walks around the fire four times, preceded by one of the Singer's assistants, who sprinkles the fragrant lotion. The patient goes out alone and faces the dawn. Inside, the Singer closes the ceremonial with a prayer, in which he asks protection from the consequence of any mistake he may have made, then he prays for everybody.

Outside, the patient stands facing the east, breathing in the dawn four times. The white man would see the yellow day coming up over miles and miles of sage, a copse of pinyon, three or four yellow pines in the soft light, distant blue swells of mountains, with here and there a volcanic cone, and very far away the snowy top of Mount Taylor.

But this is not all the Navaho sees. The sage-covered earth is Changing Woman, one of the most benevolent of the Beings, who grows old and young again with the cycle of each year's seasons. The rising sun is himself a Being who with Changing Woman produced a warrior that rid the earth of most of its evil forces and who is still using his powers to help the people. The first brightness is another Being, Dawn-Boy, and to the north, south, east and west the Navaho sees the homes of other Beings. To the north is bitter, unhappy First Woman who sends colds and sickness; to the south is the Gila Monster who helps diagnosticians reveal the unknown. The cone-shaped mountains have lava on their sides, which is the caked blood of a wicked giant killed by the Sun's warrior offspring, modern evidence of the truth of Navaho tradition. The white peak of Mount Taylor is the top of Turquoise Mountain built and decorated by the Hogan God, who later knocked its top off in a rage when he could not get the name he wanted for it and forbade any living thing to try to reach the top.

This contrast between white and Indian views of the same objects is a sample of what cultural differences mean, and the significance of value. It is true that all human beings have the same "dimensions, senses, affections and passions," but these affections and passions are not all roused by the same things, and there lie the seeds of misunderstanding and conflict imbedded in culture.

It is easy to see that a ceremonial has a powerful appeal to the emotions. From the very moment the plan to have it is conceived, suggestion goes to work on the patient and gradually increases in force. One of the principal messages is reassurance. In the preparatory period before the Singer arrives, directly and by inference the patient hears that he will be cured. When the ceremonial starts, the rituals and songs reiterate the theme in rhythm. The Singer will not permit the gossip that goes on between the movements of the ceremonial to deal with unpleasant topics. One must talk of crops and fat animals, of health and strength, and of times when people were treated by Singers and got well. The crowd is not just a crowd. It is usually composed of nearly all the people who have been of importance in the patient's life. More than that, they are the living representatives of that race of chosen people to whom the patient belongs. They are the descendants of those Navahos who first got the mystic rites from the creators of the world. All these people are gathered, their attention focused on the patient, bringing their influence and expectations to bear on his illness, their very presence inferring that powerful forces are working for his well-being. The Singer, as the mouthpiece of the Holy Beings, speaks in their voice and tells the patient that all is well. In the height of the ceremonial the patient himself becomes one of the Beings, puts his feet in their moccasins, breathes in the strength of the sun. He comes into complete harmony with the infinite, and as such must, of course, be free of all ills and evils. Of course it is very likely also that he has seen the ceremonial work with others, and may have had it before himself, in which case there will be reawakened memories and expectations of good results. The very considerable investment that the patient and his family must make in order to have the ceremonial probably contributes to the feeling that results must be obtained. The Navahos, like ourselves, develop strong faith in anything that has cost them time, money, and thought, and are reluctant to have it said that the ceremonial was after all a failure.)Very likely the sweat bath, the bath with yucca root soap, and the vomiting have important effects on the patient. It is not impossible that the medicinal herbs also have some results. Moreover, the Singer often knows the habits and tendencies of his patients in the manner of the old country doctor, and it is probable that he, like the country doctor, often gives good sound practical advice based on his knowledge of his people. In this way probably many personal and interpersonal problems become better adjusted at the time of a ceremonial.

Having shown something of their religion, and having explained that it is also their method of treating the sick, let us see what sort of obstacles it opposes to the medical treatment to which we are accustomed.

Obviously, such ceremonies, even with their herbal medicines and physical therapy, will not remove an appendix, cure tuberculosis, or prevent the participants from catching smallpox. It is in conditions of this sort, contagious diseases or surgical cases, that the Navaho method of treatment militates against the health of the people. Many times patients are kept out of a hospital so long in order to have ceremonials performed that when they come to the hospital little or nothing can be done for them. On the other hand, doctors and Navahos alike report cases where the hospital has had the first trial and has given up, and the medicine man has effected a cure.

It does not seem that Navaho theory of disease and treatment presents insurmountable obstacles to the use of white man's medical understanding and treatment, but the Navahos will have to be educated, intelligently and painstakingly, along lines of health and hygiene. It will not be necessary, nor desirable, to try to do away with Navaho religion in so doing, but the people and the practitioners will have to come to recognize the difference between the sort of illnesses that need hospital care at once and those they can care for at home, and to learn how to use their resources to produce better health. This education will probably be most effective if it is built upon the already existent beliefs and practices, rather than introduced as a totally new and different factor which has nothing to do with the "old ways" of the people.

Already a big change has taken place. Navahos come to the hospitals much more often and much earlier than formerly. The meaning hospitals have for them may be seen in the experience of one of the mission hospitals. This institution had to give up its custom of sending for patients with an ambulance and they expected that admissions would fall off considerably, at least at first, but to their surprise there was hardly any difference. The Navahos thought enough of their services to come by their own conveyances when the hospital could no longer send for them.

A little was said about the health problem in Chapter II. Much of their illness, especially in the children, is probably due to lack of proper food. Another factor is their lack of immunity to contagious diseases. They have had many epidemics of measles, mumps, chicken pox, diphtheria, influenza, and all the other diseases of childhood, which have swept over the Navahos like tidal waves, leaving deaths of children and grown people in almost every family. Since the establishment of day schools there has been a better opportunity for immunization, and no doubt this will pay dividends in the course of the years.

Tuberculosis is at present one of the chief scourges. It is so common that in some hospitals every patient is suspected of having it until X-rays show its absence. It is curious that, in a climate that is supposed to be ideal for curing tuberculosis, it should be so prevalent. Obviously, climate is only one factor, and needs the support of adequate food and not too much hard work to effect the cure. With white people, a raising of the whole standard of living, and immense amounts of propaganda concerning desirable examinations and treatment, were necessary before there was much lowering of the tuberculosis rate. Probably the same change will take place among the Navahos, but it will be harder to effect and slower to appear.

Trachoma was extremely common until recently. At present there are comparatively few cases each year, and even the former cases with scars have shown improvement under treatment with sulfanilamide.

Venereal diseases are less common than among the general population of the United States. They appear most frequently near towns and along the railroad, thinning out toward the remote sections of the Reservation. The real incidence is unknown, but Wassermann tests are done routinely in most of the hospitals and perhaps give a fair sample of the tribe. New doctors coming to the Reservation are often impressed with the lack of symptomatic syphilis, but cases of the secondary and tertiary stages occur, and there are not enough figures to say whether or not they are less common than in white hospital practice. Gonorrhea is often quite severe.

Objection to operations and other hospital procedures is said to be about the same among the Navahos as among whites. Adults are inclined to refuse to permit painful treatments for children, such as hypodermoclysis. On the whole, once a Navaho has made up his mind to let the white doctor try his art on him, he is willing to do what the doctor says. The difficulty comes in getting him to give the doctor a chance.

In addition to being a good place to immunize the Navahos, the day schools furnish an excellent starting point for health education. The teachers can do a good deal, but nurses and doctors must take a part also. Already there are classes in First Aid and child care. The possibilities are tremendous for demonstrations, clinics, talks on hygiene, and movies, such as "Another to Conquer," * but with commentary in Navaho. Some practical suggestions for doing this are included in Chapter VII.

* This is a sound moving picture designed to show the Navaho what tuberculosis means and how it should be treated. Prepared under guidance of Dr. W. W. Peter.

THE INDIAN SERVICE

THE PROBLEM OF THE NAVAHO is essentially the problem of all of us —adjustment to life. With our biological needs, our dependence on other people, our temperaments, our beliefs, and our prejudices, we must constantly adjust ourselves as best we can to a changing world. The matter is not a simple one for us nor is it for the Navahos, and no single or magic recipe has yet been found.

Medicine alone is not the answer, nor is education, religion, economics, agriculture, industry, nor radical change in patterns of behavior and belief. All these and other phases of life must be taken into consideration together.

The Navahos have serious difficulty gaining a bare subsistence; poor health drags them down; ignorance interferes with efficient use of what resources they possess; their historical experiences give them little reason to trust anybody; and the beliefs and traditions which bear them up make them distant and ultraconservative. And yet, they must adjust themselves, in a few short years, to a white civilization that was thousands of years in the making, which is infinitely complex and full of contradictions, and which, while promising wealth, surplus possessions, and numerous mechanical conveniences, also brings economic depressions and wars to the homes of the bewildered Indians.

The purpose of the Office of Indian Affairs is to help the Indians make this adjustment and the present day policies have a history that goes back beyond the eighteenth century. Before the creation of our national government, the Crown, and in some cases the colonies, assumed jurisdiction in all matters affecting trade or other relations between their own subjects and the Indians. However, neither the Crown nor any colonial government attempted to regulate the internal affairs of Indian tribes, and this pattern carried over after the creation of the United States Government. The Constitution placed in Congress two basic controls regarding Indians: (a) the power of the President, with the advice and consent of the Senate, to make treaties, and (b) the power of Congress to regulate trade with the tribes. Out of these has grown the Federal power in Indian matters as we know it today.

The Constitution presumed no authority over the lives of individual Indians. In 1832 Chief Justice Marshall formulated the legal doctrine of Indian tribal existence as visualized by the Constitution: ". . . the law of nations is, that a weaker power does not surrender its independence—its right to self-government—by associating with a stronger and taking its protection. A weak state, in order to provide for its safety, may place itself under the protection of one more powerful, without stripping itself of the right of government, and ceasing to be a state." In another decision he described an Indian tribe as a "domestic dependent nation" to distinguish it from a foreign nation.

We have travelled a long road since then and multiple functions have grown up in our relations with Indians. A few years ago in his Annual Report, the Commissioner of Indian Affairs said:

"European colonizers and their descendants brought to America ideas of land ownership, morality, government, and religion which were meaningless to the native American. In time these ideas became dominant to the exclusion of Indian habits of thought. Since we were a humane Nation and were not bent on destroying the Indians,

we assumed the responsibility of showing them how our ideas oper-
ated. We wanted them to learn our ways so that they could exist side
by side with us. In other words, we instituted a system of Indian
education which is with us today.

"We took away from the Indian all but a tiny fraction of his
wealth in land, water, and other resources, and even his food supply,
insofar as that consisted of game and wild products; and by doing so
we charged ourselves with the responsibility of keeping the Indian
from starvation. Furthermore, since the Indian's understanding of
property differed from ours, it was obvious that he would not long
retain the little property left him if he was not protected. That made
it necessary to erect trust-barriers around him which would prevent
predatory men from making off with the means by which the Indian was to be taught a new way of existing.

"By placing trust-barriers around Indian property, we exempted
his land from State and local taxation. In taking this action we
were subjecting the Indian to possible discrimination on the part of
the States which would have resulted in leaving him without health
care, education, roads, or any of the services which a State renders
its people. States and local communities cannot furnish services without revenue. Once again, then, it became necessary for the Federal
Government to assume an obligation toward the Indian tribes whose
property it was seeking to protect. . . ."

√ The Indians became, and in many cases remain, wards of the
Government. During World War I so many of them volunteered to
fight in the Army that in 1924 citizenship was conferred on all
Indians. Nevertheless, through local laws of the states of Arizona and
New Mexico, where the majority of the Navahos reside, they are
not permitted to vote because, among other things, they are under
Federal guardianship and do not pay taxes. Since they are citizens,
however, they were subject to the draft.

The headquarters for Government regulation of Navahos is located
at Window Rock, Arizona. Formerly, the reservation was divided
into six different districts, each with a complete and independent administrative organization. This led to much confusion of policy and
duplication of effort, and was abandoned in 1933 in favor of a co-

ordinated over-all management. One of the compelling needs for
the change was the serious soil erosion all over the reservation which
could be better handled if the whole area was treated as a unit than
if each of the six subdivisions had its independent and often incom-
patible ideas. Soil conservation and the control of the causes of
erosion has been a major preoccupation ever since.

Some of the factors concerned in the soil destruction began in
the middle of the nineteenth century. Before their imprisonment in
Fort Sumner, although they had some sheep, the Navahos were
largely farmers and hunters. Afterward, when allowed to return to
their lands, they were issued some sheep, and later goats and horses,
to replace losses and to help them get a fresh start. Most of the administrators of the period held the belief that quantity expansion and
exploitation of nature was the way to prosperity, and so they urged
the Navahos to increase their flocks. The Navahos complied with
such enthusiasm that in a few years time their flocks had outgrown
the ability of the country to feed them and at the same time maintain its plant cover.

As the range became overgrazed the water which fell on the surface and which should have been caught and held by surface growth,
swept down the steep slopes and cut deep arroyos. Some of these
stretched for more than a hundred miles, cutting the bottoms out of
fertile valleys. The damage, once started, was accelerated by every
storm, and wind. In time these washes and gullies cutting down
below the surface drained away sub-surface waters which, added to
the scanty rainfall, caused the perennial grasses to dry out while
hardier but less useful weeds took their place. This went on over
thousands of square miles as the Navahos moved their sheep, goats,
and horses into the more remote reaches of the country set aside for
them.

In order to preserve some animals alive, it has been necessary to
bring about drastic reductions in the number of sheep and other
stock. While this has caused widespread hardship and suffering, it
is evident that in the long run it will benefit the Indians. A careful
study of the facts indicates that overpopulation was one important
reason why in recent years the sheep's wool has been poor and the

lambs light. By reducing the number of animals on the range, the same amount of fodder can produce better sheep and thus raise the income.

Therefore, concomitant with the reduction in numbers, there has been an effort to improve breed and breeding practices. The tribe has spent considerable money buying good rams which are rented out to individual owners, and the Government has established a laboratory at Fort Wingate to experiment with developing the best type of sheep for the range, for the uses of the Navahos, and for the commercial market.

Moreover, a livestock disposition project was established to make it possible for the Navahos to sell their poor quality sheep, which commercial buyers would not take and which pulled down the quality of the flock if kept and used for breeding. These sheep are bought for a reasonable price and sold as fresh meat locally or canned for use in reservation schools and hospitals. While not profitable commercially, the meat is nevertheless perfectly good nutritionally, and has been of great help in improving the diet in government institutions where meat was otherwise too costly to be frequently served.

Actual results of the various efforts can be seen in these figures assembled in 1943:

Since 1931, Navaho sheep reduced from 575,000 to 433,000
Since 1931, Navaho lambs *increased* from 317,000 to 346,000
Since 1931, weight of lambs increased from 53 to over 60 lbs.
Since 1931, weight of fleece increased from less than 4 to 6 lbs.
Since 1931, if wool is worth 30¢ and lambs worth 10¢ a pound, the value of these products increased from $2,126,747 to $2,861,236.

In spite of these figures, the Navahos do not yet recognize very thoroughly the need and benefits in stock reduction and the program has encountered severe opposition. Many still feel that their means of livelihood is being stolen from them, that they are being pushed around, and that they know much better how to raise sheep from years of practice than the men in Window Rock or the other offices who "don't even own sheep." (In this reaction the Navahos do not differ from popular attitudes to conservation measures of all sorts as seen all over the country.) Some Navahos are cooperative and in the course of time it is probable that all will see the benefits. Unfortunately, the ill feeling attached to stock reduction has spread to other Government activities, so that school, medical care, and all other contacts have suffered at times.

In order to carry out the reduction program, the reservation, which had just been consolidated from the six independent divisions, was re-divided into 18 districts. All are now under the head office at Window Rock but a District Supervisor is in charge of each district and represents the General Superintendent locally. The District Supervisor is responsible for the carrying out of Government programs in his district with the exception of education, health, and construction, but even here there is, or should be, close collaboration. His duties, therefore, include administrative relations with Indians, law and order, work programs on farm, range, and livestock, distribution of relief, selective service, and rationing. His principal aids are the Range Riders who have most of the direct contact with the Indians.

The District Supervisor is expected to do everything he can to increase Indian participation in the programs. This succeeds in varying degrees in different districts, being most successful where the members of the District Council (elected by local residents) are sympathetic to the aims of the Government. At present (1943), two of the eighteen Supervisors, and eleven of the twenty Range Riders are themselves Navahos.

The Farm Program is mostly restricted to the irrigated areas, where Indians are supervised in their use of water, and encouraged to improve their farming practices. No control is exercised over other farms, beyond requiring a permit for breaking uncultivated ground.

Relief is furnished as rations, and never in amounts sufficient to entirely support an individual or family. It supplements where necessary an otherwise insufficient subsistence. Cases on relief have decreased markedly since wage work and checks from soldiers have become general. In September 1942 there were 3,570 persons who received some relief; in September 1943 only 528 persons were aided.

The overall soil conservation program is linked with the school system. Much emphasis is placed, especially in the high schools, on the need for and methods of saving the soil from further destruction.

Education for Navaho children started in a day school which soon became a boarding school at Fort Defiance after the return from Fort Sumner. Eventually other boarding schools were built in different parts of the reservation, but many of the children were taken as far away as Pennsylvania and California. In these schools there were children from many tribes, from parts of the country with different climatic conditions and ways of making a living. Consequently, not much could be done in teaching the children of each tribe how to get along best with its particular conditions. Instead they were taught as if they were white children and would always live in white communities. Ninety-five per cent of the children went home and entered a life for which their education had given them little preparation and many handicaps. Moreover, the schools in which they had spent their early years had been much like orphan asylums, and had deprived them of the many advantages to character formation afforded by family life in even the poorest Indian home.

In recent times, there has been an attempt to adapt the boarding schools on the reservation to present-day needs by making two of them Vocational High Schools, and a third an Agricultural High School where students can get practical instruction that will help them in life under reservation conditions if they are unable to leave. Instruction is also offered in the usual academic courses, and in types of work that will enable them to support themselves in white society if they wish to do so and it becomes possible. The other five boarding schools limit instruction to six or eight grades.

In addition there are almost fifty day schools scattered over the reservation. These have become important community centers where the children learn, the parents use the laundry, bathing, and shop facilities, and where various specialists such as doctors, nurses, and home economics teachers give demonstrations, and meet otherwise inaccessible people. Before the war children were brought to school

Photograph by Helen M. Post

A Shepherdess Taking Her Flock out to Graze

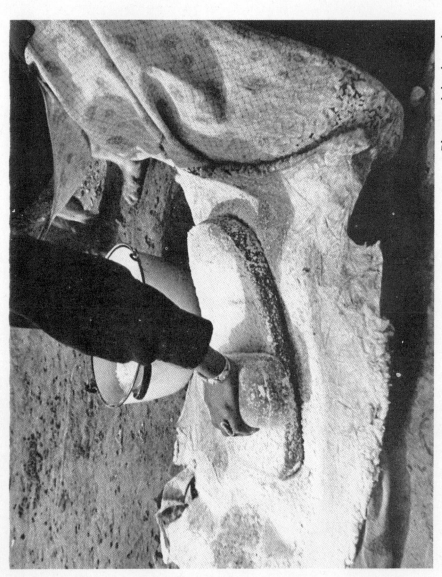

Grinding Corn to Flour by Hand

A Mother Makes Bread for Supper

Photograph by the authors

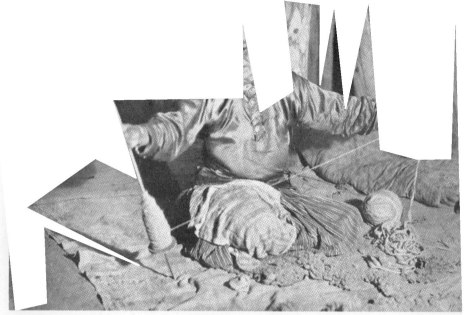

Photograph by Helen M. Post

Woman Spinning Wool into Yarn for a Rug

Photograph by the authors

Weaving a Navaho Rug

daily by bus. Since gas, tires, busses, and repair parts have become so scarce, an experiment is being made of having the children stay at the day school from Monday through Friday, sleeping in simple buildings nearby. A number of children also attend Mission boarding schools, both on and off the reservation, and a much smaller number go to Government schools away from the reservation.

Many children attend school for only two or three years, but an increasing number are continuing to the higher grades or high school, and a few go to college. Although, legally, it is a punishable offense to keep children from school, the law is not enforced. The following table shows the proportion in and out of school:

SCHOOL ATTENDANCE OF NAVAHO CHILDREN AGED 6-18

	Number in Navaho Service schools '42-43	Estimated number, all schools	Estimated number of children	Percentage in school
6-12 yrs. of age				
Day-school	1789	1995		
Boarding School	1320	2008		
Total	3109	4003	8285	49%
13-18 yrs. of age				
Day-school	262	353		
Boarding School	1102	1406		
Total	1364	1759	6215	28%
Total, all ages	4473	5762	14,500	40%

The education given in the day schools is not so intense as in the boarding schools, but it is probably more extensive since many more persons, both old and young, attend or have contact with the day schools than with the boarding schools.

AVERAGE DAILY ADULT ATTENDANCE FOR EDUCATIONAL ACTIVITIES 1942-43

	At boarding schools	At day schools	Total
Men	48.2	310.9	359.1
Women	59.5	426.1	485.6
Total	107.7	737.0	844.7

It would seem that the best hope of raising the general level of literacy in the tribe is the day school.

A large and important branch of the Navaho Service is that which deals with health, and in it lies one of the best means of establishing better collaboration between the Indians and our white society. Illness is a matter of much concern to the Navaho, and he is perhaps more willing to try new methods of healing than new methods of raising sheep.

Hospital facilities are excellent, and are being used increasingly. The largest hospital is at Fort Defiance, where there are 250 beds, 100 of which are for tuberculous patients. Other smaller hospitals, each with an outpatient clinic, are located at Shiprock, Crownpoint, Fort Wingate, Winslow, Chinle, Tuba City, and Tohatchi. In addition, there is a fifty-bed tuberculosis sanitarium at Kayenta. Before the war, several of these hospitals had two doctors and a good deal of field work was possible, but now Fort Defiance is the only hospital with more than one physician.

The limited field work done at present amounts to examination and immunization of day school pupils by the doctor from the nearest hospital; examination and treatment of other patients who meet him at the schools on these trips; and occasional visits by specialists to the boarding schools. The field program is the one most in need of expansion and the day schools offer an excellent starting point for demonstrations and education in health matters.

The Government has also taken a hand in organizing the tribe politically. It will be remembered that in the first chapter we said that originally there was no one leader of the whole Navaho tribe but there were a number of men who stood out from the rest for their force of character and who served as leaders for smaller or larger numbers of their people, usually their clansmen. This sort of leadership depended entirely on group support, and if the individual fell into disfavor for any reason his leadership vanished. The Government was slow to recognize this state of affairs in its early contact with the Navahos, and dealt with men who were only self-appointed leaders but who were amenable to the Government's ideas. There were even attempts to create tribal leaders by executive order when the existing chiefs refused to cooperate. Of course such "ersatz" leaders had little or no control over their people, but years of this policy came close to wrecking the whole tradition of head-man-ship, and the family or family group seemed to develop as the principal unit showing strong cooperation and leadership.

In 1923 an attempt was made to remedy the situation by creating a Navaho Council. Largely because its members were simply care-fully selected "yes-men" who did not represent the tribe, nothing came of the effort. In 1925 small units were decreed within the tribe known as "chapters," each about the size of a township, and they were instructed to elect certain officers and to handle their local business through them. It was a technique quite unfamiliar to the Indians, and not very satisfactory, but it gave them some experience in handling elections and finding out how various men among them behaved in public office. These efforts, and those that followed were attempts to have the tribe develop some organization that would enable it to deal with its growing intra-tribal problems, with other Indians, and with white men. In 1937 a set of rules and regulations of election and procedure for the Council was drawn up, and after its approval in 1938 by the Secretary of the Interior, it became the basis for the present tribal government.

According to these Rules, the Council has 74 members, the num-ber of representatives from each district depending on the popula-tion. These men are elected for a four-year term, and meet two or three times a year. As it operates at present, the Council passes on expenditure of tribal funds; defines conditions of tribal member-ship; regulates the domestic relations of Navahos, including mar-riage, divorce, and inheritance; and administers justice. The Coun-cil also expresses opinions regarding Government acts and advises the Government.

While this type of self-rule has not yet entirely proved itself, it has come nearer the mark than any previous effort, and gives evi-dence of possessing spontaneity, the will to survive and to speak for the tribe. The idea of reservation-wide tribal government is finding acceptance and it will probably grow in flexibility and responsive-ness as time goes on. The indications are that the individual mem-bers are more and more reporting to their communities and obtain-ing validation or refutation of their decisions in Council. Education for self-government, both in the schools and in adult classes, would very likely bring the time nearer when the Navahos will be running their own affairs.

One important phase of government in which the Navahos have a large share is the administration of justice. Except for major crimes, all offenses committed on the reservation and which cannot be settled privately are tried before a court composed of three Navaho judges, or in some cases associate judges. They observe a code of laws which was adopted in 1937, and take tribal custom into account in making decisions. Under some circumstances there are provisions for calling a jury. A group of Navaho policemen who travel about the reservation maintain order and enforce the law; one of their chief duties is to control traffic in liquor, therefore they nearly always appear at the public ceremonials, where drinking frequently takes place. The most frequent causes of arrest are drunkenness and domestic difficulties. Sentences for misconduct consist of fines, or alternatively a number of days in jail corresponding to each dollar of the fine. Four jails are maintained on the reservation and the prisoners do much useful work while serving their sentences.

The head of the Law and Order organization is white, but for the rest, this branch of Navaho government seems to be more nearly self-government than any of the others. Even better results could be expected if time were spent training the judges, and if more money were provided for policemen's salaries so that men of a higher educational level would be attracted to the work.

The Navaho tribe and the Government have set up a number of projects known collectively as "tribal enterprises." Two of these have already been mentioned in the discussion of stock improvement, namely the Livestock Disposition project and the Livestock Improvement project. The largest and most important of the undertakings from the commercial point of view is the sawmill located on the plateau above Fort Defiance. Large ponderosa pines that are ripe or over-ripe are harvested scientifically so that the forest is not depleted. Many thousand board-feet of lumber are milled from the trees, helping supply building materials for the war effort and work opportunities for the Indians. The mill is managed by white foremen but profits revert to tribal funds.

Another enterprise of potential importance is the Arts and Crafts Guild. This organization is devoted to improving the standards of workmanship for weaving and silverwork, seeing that craftsmen get a better return for their products, and finding and developing a dependable, high-class market for the goods. The war has caused a decline in the amount of handicrafts produced, but probably it will revive later.

Finally there is the flour mill at Round Rock which was established in the center of the wheat-growing area of the reservation to give the Indians an opportunity to have their wheat processed near home and to provide a market.

All of these projects have aided the Navaho economy. It remains now to find trained and capable Navahos to take over their operation for the future. Perhaps the best source of such managers will be the men returning from the armed forces at the close of the war.

In addition to these industries, certain natural resources on the reservation are leased by the tribe to commercial operators who employ many Navahos. Such resources include coal, oil, helium, vanadium, and copper. A few individual Indians own and operate small coal mines.

To keep both Governmental services and tribal activities going, a considerable amount of work has to be done in the way of supervising, planning, keeping up roads and communications, and keeping records. For example, "communications" includes a network of telephone lines to all day schools and to other Government stations; and the Roads Division has about 3,290 miles of road to maintain and improve; the Traders Relations Division sees to licensing traders on the reservation, investigates complaints about them, helps with the new Indian cooperatives, and keeps records of the volume and type of business between traders and Navahos as an index of the economic state of the tribe.

The plans and the goals of the Navaho Service are excellent, and one cannot help being moved with admiration, but it must be remembered that although much has been accomplished a great deal is still in the form of intention rather than realization. Every step forward is achieved with great difficulty. There is the conservative resistance of the Indians and there is the indifference or active (if covert) hostility to the Government program on the part of some of its employees although numerous others work effectively toward accomplishment of the aims. Frequent misunderstandings occur because of cultural and language differences between Indians and whites. There is political pressure, or the threat of pressure, from individuals who want to get the Indian land, who are opposed to Indian cooperatives, who want to keep the Indian standard of living low so that labor will be cheap and profit greater on articles of trade, and who want to cut down the Federal money spent on Indians. There are also people who mean well for the Indians, but who attack the Government's program because they wish the Indian christianized and forget that freedom of religion is not limited to Christians. They would have Indian education carried out in mission schools with only financial aid from the Government, thereby depriving the Indian of the rights embodied in the non-sectarian public schools which other Americans can attend. These attacks and interferences are not well balanced by other forces, because the Navahos are unable to vote and because the general public pays little attention to the Indian problem and leaves the field clear for those who are in it for the special reasons already mentioned.

The war has added a widespread general curtailment of all Government projects and an increase rather than a decrease in the pressure that would take things away from the Indians. This is in spite of the fact that the Navahos are in the Army, the Navy, and the Marines, and doing a job for their country just the same as everyone else.

It is to be hoped that some of the optimistic plans for the post-war world will materialize for the greater happiness of a greater number of people and for the reduction in the number and scale of wars. Experience shows that over-all schemes, however well they may appear when laid out on paper, are usually unwieldy and compete poorly with established customs and habits. Progress is more sure when it occurs by expansion from small practical demonstrations of successful operation. For this reason, the administrative performance of such a comparatively small organization as the Navaho Service may have much wider significance if it proves itself a useful model of human management, and inter-racial relations.

NAVAHO WAYS AND WHITE MAN'S
MEDICINE — IN THE HOSPITAL

IN THE PRECEDING CHAPTERS an attempt has been made to supply general information about Navahos and the Navaho Service. The present chapter is an effort to show by specific instances how this material can be used in working with the Navahos in a practical way.

Because the authors are physicians and because the health problem among the Navahos seems to be one of the most important problems, the next pages are devoted to discussion that will be most useful to doctors and nurses and other medical workers. Many teachers, range riders, and even construction men will be called at times to render medical assistance, or to try to persuade some sick Indian to go to the hospital, and so they, too, may find the suggestions helpful.

It is true that the type of ceremonial described in the chapter on religion will not heal tuberculosis, remove an appendix, or set a broken bone. However, the greatest single aid to recovery from illness is rest, and things which occupy the mind and keep up hope enable one to accept affliction more easily. Few people will doubt that the attitude of a patient is one of the most important factors in his recovery. Even when good medical attention is available, time, rest, and a hopeful attitude play leading roles, and they are all the more important to the many cases of sickness among the Navahos that never come to the attention of doctors, since there are not enough hospital beds to care for all.

Because of their beliefs, the Indians have a strong tendency to try their own ceremonials before calling in a white doctor, regardless of the type of sickness. As we have suggested, the Navaho theory of illness is not that illness is caused by germs, wrong food, or improper functioning of the body, as we believe, but rather that by some means the patient fell out of harmony with the forces of nature, and this discord makes him susceptible to catching a sickness from another person, breaking his leg, or developing any of the symptoms that can plague a human being. The natural consequence of this belief is that, when a person falls ill, the most important thing is to restore through ritual the harmony which has been disrupted so the body can heal itself.

The primary concern of the Navaho is with the illness, and getting rid of it, and he does not demand consistency of theory and treatment so long as the illness is dispelled. He is remarkably experimental and practical in his attitude and often tries medical preparations dispensed by Government workers or bought at the traders' before arranging a ceremonial, to see if the medicine is as good as the white people tell him. Similarly, if he tries a ceremonial first and it is not effective he is likely to come to the hospital.

The Navahos know from experience that it is possible to catch diseases from people who have them. The time of the following incident, cited as an example, must have been about 1870-1880.

"One day a man and a woman came to our place. The man was pretty sick. He was my brother. His wife went home and he stayed there. Next day when they were looking at this man, the people says he has something all over his body. What he has over his body is all red. We had stayed all night with him, all of us. In the morning my father took us to another place. Father says it was pretty bad to stay near that man, we might get it from him. What he had on his body was getting heavier every day. They found out it was smallpox. My father got afraid to go over to him, but my mother wasn't afraid.

She went over and took care of him. After she stayed with him two days, we heard she got it, too. The sick man and my mother and my father was the only ones talked together. When my mother came over she just walked behind the doorway here and talked to us. My father told her not to come in. Some of our folks fixed some food up and carried it outside for them. The man got better but my mother got worse. She got too worse, had sores all over her body and died, didn't live long. Everybody got afraid to go near there, so they didn't bury her but just left her inside the brush hogan. They cut a lot of pinyon limbs and cover her up good with it and close up the brush hogan. We move away from there right away.

"One of my oldest brothers, he was a Singer, too, came in there just about the time my mother died, and he got it right away. But he didn't have it very bad and got better. The two men used some kind of medicine, and was drinking it and rubbing it on their bodies, and they got well. But they don't come in on us. They keep their camp on one side. They do that for quite a while till they think they are sure well."

One could hardly improve on the precautions that the Navahos took in this situation.

When it comes to the hospitalization of Navahos, one sometimes meets with a surprising amount of resistance. It is well to bear in mind that the Indians' experience with hospitals extends over a period of less than one lifetime. Only recently have they brought in a patient before he was moribund; they commonly hold the opinion that a hospital is a place to go to die. A generation ago this was the view of most people in our culture and it still is the view of many people today. Moreover, it is hard for most of us to picture the extent of personal adjustment that a Navaho must make when he becomes a bed patient in a hospital. When we go to a hospital we may have to get used to eating our meals at a different hour from our usual one, or to having our faces washed for us, or taking medicine we do not like, or the various medical and surgical procedures that one goes to the hospital to get, but the Navaho has these adjustments and many more to make. He is unaccustomed to a bed, to living by the clock, to staying in one place continuously instead of wandering around as he pleases, and to efficient impersonal attention by people whose language he cannot speak. He cannot see why he must be content with gruel and milk when, if he were home, he would be fed as much as he could eat of the best food the family could get for him. He feels uneasy about doing intimate personal things before other people, especially people who are not related or familiar. It seems as if the doctors and nurses could not be very much interested in him because they come to see him only at long intervals instead of staying with him constantly as his family would. He cannot understand why if medicine is going to cure him, they do not give it to him all the time instead of only a little three or four times a day. When he has been sick at home before and has had a ceremonial, the medicine man has given him his undivided attention constantly for as much as nine days and nights. There were numbers of other people there, too, all laboring to get him well. Here it seems as if no one cares whether he gets well or not, and all he has to do is to lie there and wonder what his family is doing, and feel homesick for them and for his hogan and mutton.

The patient would think it silly and out of place for a white doctor to put on a dance for him or pray over him or construct religious paraphernalia, but he would be much easier in his mind if the doctor would explain a little about the kind of sickness he has and what white people believe to be the best way of treating it. This is a wonderful opportunity for health education, for if the doctor is able to convince the patient that rest is the principal thing his body needs to get well, for instance, or that soft foods are easier for his stomach to digest when he is sick than mutton, he is likely to follow such a regimen next time he gets sick whether he comes to the hospital or not. That is, he will follow it if it works. Otherwise, he will probably conclude that this time the white doctor guessed wrongly as to what was the matter with him and how it should be treated, just as the native diagnosticians sometimes do, and he will go to another doctor, either white or Indian. Each patient must be thought of as an educational problem as well as a therapeutic one.

Explanations cannot be simply a list of technical terms which even the interpreter cannot understand or translate. They must be in simple, graphic words with as much reference as possible to things familiar to the Indians. They have a fair knowledge of human anatomy and even better of sheep and goat anatomy. As can be seen from the description of the smallpox epidemic quoted above, they also have a good idea of contagiousness, although they do not always act on it.

Medical workers should be aware of Navaho customs and attitudes that have a direct bearing on hospitalization: When a man or woman gets sick, the family takes over the direction of treatment. Sometimes the patient has a voice in the matter, but not always. The family decides whether to call a Singer or a diagnostician or take the patient to the hospital. If the Singer comes they tell him just what they want him to do. A few medicine men take it on themselves to advise the family, but most conform to the pattern of doing as they are told with all the skill they possess. In dealing with the hospitalization of a patient it is important to keep this in mind, as persuading the patient may be only the first step in securing your result, and when the family is considering a matter, it may take several hours of talking to reach a decision.

The patient and his family are principally interested in the present illness, especially the present complaint. In their thinking, they recognize clearly enough the possibility of connection between past and present illness, but, because of the customs of their own diagnosticians and Singers, they look on it as weakness on the part of the doctor to ask questions. They think he should know what is wrong and get to work fixing it. This raises an obstacle to getting an adequate past history. The Indian patient will usually respond to the doctor if he devotes enough time and interest to the description of his present illness. Even if the chief complaint has little to do with the fundamental pathology, it is worth while to give some symptomatic treatment, such as liniment or cough medicine, to indicate that you take it seriously. By making this concession one can often carry out procedures that would be resisted otherwise, and the patient will be much more contented, for he will see that what bothered him is being treated.

Most Navahos like to make speeches. "Yes" and "No" answers are not customary with them. A busy doctor or nurse is often irritated when, on asking a patient how long he has been sick, he starts a detailed account of how he has passed the last two days. Although this may sound irrelevant at the start, if one listens, the patient usually ends up with a point which has considerable bearing on his previous account and gives it meaning. If one does not listen, the patient will not talk and the medical worker will not learn anything.

The Navahos are accused of being unresponsive. It is true that they do not often say thank you, nor show much enthusiasm when something is done that they like. Such behavior is not good formal manners in the Navaho way. In unfamiliar surroundings one must maintain an outward dignity and composure. A part of this behavior is often dictated by shyness. Even with each other, children returning to school in the fall act like strangers until they get re-acquainted. It is unlikely that the outward appearance is a true indication of the inward feeling.

If you have occasion to drive up to a Navaho hogan, you might be surprised that your friends do not rush up to shake your hands. They may not even act as if they knew you were there, or they may retire into the hogan. After a little some of them will probably approach you to see what you want or to ask you inside. You get a different picture if you are living with the family and in the hogan when another car is approaching. Every one quits what he is doing so as to be able to hear better. There are excited whisperings. The children are sent to peek out the cracks to see who it is, and when that is not good enough, one may be sent out to throw some trash on the ash pile so he can get a better view. Even if this report discloses that it is some favorite relative, calm has descended by the time he comes in, hands are shaken gravely, and some minutes are spent in silent smoking before a word beyond that of greeting is said.

Your tone of voice and attitude will tell the Navahos a great deal, no matter what words you use, even if they understand no English. They are very keen judges of whether or not you are friendly, patient, interested. They may misunderstand if you talk too loudly or too rapidly, as they may take that to indicate irritation whether or not you feel it. You will get far with them if you are friendly and patient, and nowhere if you are not.

The patient in the hospital is likely to feel lonesome away from his family surroundings and may want to leave on that account. If he is too sick to do this safely, a compromise that has been used successfully is to put him in a private room and get a member of his family to come and stay with him. This gives the doctor an added opportunity for educating Navahos in medical matters.

Navahos like to eat heartily and to feel satisfied after eating. They think this is more important if they are sick than when they are well, and sometimes will want to leave the hospital because they dislike a liquid diet. If you find out about this and feel the patient still needs hospitalization, you may be able to keep him by compromising and putting him on semi-solid food. It is very easy for the patients to misunderstand special diets and assume them to be mere slop and evidence of neglect.

Navaho women are very modest. They are trained from the time they begin to walk that they must keep their skirts down and their bodies covered below the waist. The upper part of the body does not seem to matter so much. Nurses should be even more careful with them than with white patients not to expose them unnecessarily when bathing, giving douches, or enemas.

Like most people, the Navahos do not want to be laughed at unless they are trying to be funny. Among nearly all American Indians, ridicule and public opinion were extremely potent forces in producing smoothly running community life. These forces worked so well that little was needed in the way of policing or formal regulations for punishment. Even today, most Indians, especially those who live largely according to their own customs, are more sensitive to ridicule than the average white man. They care most about the opinions of other Indians, but next to this they want to be well regarded by those white people they look upon as their friends. On the other hand, the Navahos have an excellent sense of humor and love to make jokes, especially puns, in their own language. Much of their humor is quite subtle and based on the vagaries of human nature.

In general Navahos have an uneasy feeling about people who show some physical deformity. This may be related to their fear of witchcraft and result in their thinking that since such a person cannot do very much because of the deformity, he may try to exert power or gain riches in an abnormal way. Their fear is probably in part due to feeling that since the deformed are out of harmony with the forces of nature, contact with them may bring disharmony to one's own life, according to the general principles of contagious magic. Occasionally a deformed infant will be abandoned to die, or will be brought to the hospital and never taken home again. Their uneasiness is doubtless also linked with their admiration of physical perfection, a point of view said to have been dictated by the Holy Beings. In the ceremonials where Navahos take the part of the various gods, there is a strict injunction against the parts being played by any but the physically perfect. Probably this ruling prevented transmission of disease through the leather masks used in certain ceremonials, in spite of the prevalence a few years ago of trachoma. People with sore eyes were not allowed to wear the masks.

Many Navahos do not like to speak about their past illnesses, or to mention relatives who have died, for fear that such talk will start trouble again. Often at a Blessing Way ceremonial, for instance, the Singer will put a stop to bad news or tales of hardship, saying they must speak of success with crops, lots of rain, and things recognized by all as good. This is sometimes an added difficulty in getting a good past history or family history, but the passage of time and the growth of confidence in the hospital will frequently overcome the feeling. At other times a long-term acquaintance with the person and his family is the only way of knowing what his health history has been.

Navaho babies usually continue to nurse until the next baby is born. This is contrary to our idea of what is desirable, but it must be remembered that the child probably has no other source of milk and there is little opportunity for gradation between infant food and the adult diet of fried bread and meat. With white people it is more consideration for the mother than the child that puts an end to nursing at six to nine months. Thus, when either the mother or the infant is sick, both may have to be accepted by the hospital, perhaps a sick baby and his source of food, or a not too sick mother and her hungry child.

In their native medicine, Navahos use herbal concoctions by first rubbing them on their bodies, beginning at the feet and working up to the head in a ceremonial sequence, and then by drinking what is left over. Consequently, at some of the hospitals it has been found helpful to provide liniment for use on the outside of the body when giving internal medication.

The Navahos are accustomed to ointments. In the windy spring months they often smear their faces with sheep tallow and red clay to prevent chapping. Skin diseases are treated with various greases. In the ceremonials, ointments from such animals as the mountain lion are often used. Skunk grease has been recommended as a small-pox preventive. Thus, they will accept readily any sort of ointment if it is explained to them, and will use it as directed if directions are sufficiently specific.

Doctors have reported seeing cases brought to the hospital in which chest pain had already been treated with applications of various kinds of pitch, probably as a counterirritant or poultice. Emetics and cathartics are used often in ceremonials "to clean out the body." Astringents such as juniper tea are used after childbirth to "clean the blood." Medicines are also employed as inhalants, usually by sprinkling a pinch on a red coal while the patient leans over and breathes the fumes. This practice paves the way for using inhalations in such conditions as croup and bronchitis, and may be carried out quite easily in hogans.

The Navahos are accustomed to doing things connected with treating the sick in a precise way, as prescribed by the medicine man, and with certain items always following certain other items. This gives the doctor a basis for having treatments carried out exactly as he wishes, provided he makes that wish very clear and definite and avoids all vague and generalized recommendations.

With their own medicines the Navahos are always interested in what sort of plant, animal or mineral mixture they are using, and how the components were collected and prepared. They would take white medicine more seriously if the doctor were to describe a little

A Navaho Singer and Some of His Materials for Performing a Curing Ceremonial

Photograph by Helen M. Post

The Fire Dance

the source of the various elements in his doses, making the picture vivid but nontechnical.

To the Navahos the number four is charged with great significance. This may be related to the four points of the compass, or the four seasons of the year, but in any event carries emotional tones which are possibly similar to those felt in Europe during the middle ages for the number three and its association with the Trinity. The doctor treating Navahos can use four in a number of ways to fortify treatment, such as prescribing medicine four times a day, courses of treatment in groups of four days, and bed rest for four days, or four weeks, or twice four days.

Bathing by means of the sweatbath or the yucca-root-and-water bath is part of both ceremonial and everyday treatment. Sweatbaths are taken to tone up the system, as well as for purposes of cleanliness, and after a doctor has seen or participated in one, so that he understands what it involves, he might find it very helpful to advise it in certain cases where he feels a general tonic is needed. Nurses and day school teachers report that if you provide a Navaho with soap and water there is no trouble in keeping him clean. When given the facilities, Navahos love to bathe, and at home it seems that only the lack of water and privacy keeps them from it. As with the use of liniment, the ceremonial bathing order begins with the feet and works up toward the head.

All through the hospitalization, and even after the doctor tells the patient he may go home, the Navaho may have been feeling that he should not have come to the hospital without at least trying out the medicine man first. He may believe that the cure will only be temporary without the religious sanctions procured through the ceremonial. In many cases such feelings get too strong for him and he will leave the hospital in spite of the doctor's pleading. If the doctor could find this out before the patient makes this decision, it would often be possible to persuade him to wait until the doctor is finished with him. One might tell him, for instance, that he now has a white man's sickness and needs white man's medicine, or suggest that he have a Sing after the doctor at the hospital has treated him.

Nothing will be gained by treating his feelings lightly, any more than if you tried to tell a good Christian or Jew in a hospital that seeing the minister will have no effect on his recovery. The Christian, the Jew, and the Navaho have a deeply rooted conviction that unless their religious needs are taken care of as well as their physical needs, they are not truly cured. One difference between the Christian and the Navaho is that the minister and priest have modified their procedures so that they can be used in the hospital to the comfort of the patient's soul, while the Navaho medicine man has not yet done this and has received no encouragement to do so from the white doctors or administrators.

It is impossible to say what might be gained by according to the medicine men the same privileges and respect that we give priests and ministers. Perhaps no use would be made of them, because the whole hospital atmosphere would seem inimical to Navaho religious concepts. Certainly it would be impractical in most cases to attempt to have ceremonials performed in the hospital building. It seems, however, as if a great deal could be done in the way of improving relations with the medicine men and thereby with Navaho patients if the medicine men were treated as colleagues to some extent, shown how a hospital operates, allowed to witness operations so as to see for themselves that much training is necessary. They have already given evidence of their interest in such things by their attendance at first-aid classes, and their eagerness to take and use a clinical thermometer when it is permitted. It would be better to teach them our medical theories and some of our practices than to have them pick them up in a distorted form from uncontrolled sources.

One way in which the medicine man could be of definite help to a doctor would be to persuade a patient who wanted to go home to stay until the hospital was through with him before having a ceremonial. If medicine men were used much in this way the hospitals or patients would have to pay them something for their time, because they are often busy men with families to support. They would do this sort of talking only if a good relationship could be established between them and the hospital or the doctor. Perhaps they could be asked to perform some of the very short curing rites that are taken from longer ceremonials, or to suggest to the patient that he have a

Blessing Way ceremonial after leaving. As far as the lay Navaho is concerned, the white doctor or nurse is just another sort of medicine man, who uses different but not necessarily better techniques to attain the same end, namely, the healing of the sick.

The good medicine man is usually very intelligent, but a difficulty will lie in distinguishing between the good ones and those less gifted and less admirable. It is altogether likely that there are some who would try to use a relationship with the hospital for their personal aggrandizement rather than as a means of helping their people. Men of this sort would become obvious in time, but in any case the harm they might do would be greatly outweighed by the good to be expected from a gradual infiltration of improved hygienic ideals and practices.

It is not just the medicine men who should be educated; perhaps because of their intelligence they could be taught more than the others, but all Navahos need health education, and will get it from everything they see a doctor or nurse do or refrain from doing. Each explanation you take pains to make will spread like a ripple in a pool, for the Navahos love to tell a "story," and they are all keenly interested in health. It is well to remember that they will tell it as they understand it, so that it is worth some pains to see that their understanding is the same as yours.

Having said this much about the importance of explanation, a few samples will be given below to serve as a guide in developing such techniques. These are not intended to be memorized and repeated verbatim, but only to show some of the possibilities.

The first thing to make sure of is your interpreters, since you are dependent on them for knowing what Navahos say to you and for speaking to Navahos. It is worth a good deal of your time to train the interpreters so that they know your ways of expressing things, and understand what you are talking about. Good interpretation requires considerable intelligence, depends on knowing the person for whom one is interpreting and knowing the subject under discussion. Several of the medical interpreters who attended the school held for them at Fort Defiance considered that they got the greatest help from the detailed discussions they had in trying to find the right word to express an idea. In doing this they learned a great deal about medical concepts that had previously been unknown to them.

Interpreting is hard enough between any two languages, and is far more than just finding equivalent words; you have to find ways of expressing the idea and the feeling that goes with it. With Navaho and English the problem is further complicated by the fact that the words are used in a different order so that a sentence has to be turned around before being translated; and in telling a story, the Navaho is likely to start with the point and then explain what led up to it, whereas in English the point comes at the end.

The doctor, teacher, or other worker speaking through an interpreter should first have clearly in mind what he wants to say, and then he should reduce it to the simplest possible English. If he works customarily with the same interpreter, he should listen to the interpreter's English and use the same expressions as much as possible, because that will make it more understandable to the interpreter and thus the translation will be more accurate. Too much cannot be said in favor of workers among the Navahos trying to learn some Navaho words so that they can follow the general drift of the discussion.*

In the examples following, the English used is similar to that employed by the interpreter with whom the writers were most familiar.

PNEUMONIA. "This patient has a sickness in his lungs. Some pus is in his lungs and it is filling them up. That is why he has to breathe so fast. It is harder for him to get his breath because there is pus in his lungs. This kind of sickness goes pretty fast and is pretty bad unless he gets just the right kind of treatment. I am glad that you brought him in so soon after he got sick, because we have some good medicine that helps a man with his sickness a whole lot. If he comes into the hospital right away he will probably be much

---

* The Medical Dictionary, that was worked out by the medical interpreters, the medical staff, and Mr. Adolf Bitanny. is worth study so that you can familiarize yourself with medical terminology in Navaho. A copy can be obtained from the medical office at Window Rock.

Learning Navaho, by Father Berard Haile, St. Michaels 1941, is also a good text for a beginner.

better in four days and all right in twice four days. If you take him home he will probably get sicker all the time, and he will die pretty soon. See, here are some X-rays. This one shows you a man with good lungs, nothing wrong with them. Here is the X-ray of the patient. You can see his picture has a big white place in it. That is where the pus is. If we treat him in the hospital, that place will get smaller and smaller until his lungs get to look just like these good ones. You ought to leave him in the hospital until they look good again.

"Would you like to listen to the sick place through this rubber that I use? (stethoscope). First listen to this other man's lungs. Can you hear what it sounds like when he takes a big breath? Now put the rubber right here (over consolidation). That sounds different, doesn't it? The pus that is in there, that makes the white place in the X-ray, makes it sound like that. When he gets well that place will sound just like that other man's lung. You ought to leave him in the hospital until it sounds good again."

TUBERCULOSIS. "This boy has tuberculosis. I guess you know about tuberculosis? Has he been coughing for a long time? Has he been getting poor (thin) for a long time? Did he ever spit any blood? Did he ever have any fever? I think he has had it quite a while, and I will show you why. See, here are some X-rays. This one is from a boy who has good lungs, nothing the matter with them. You can see they look all the same. Here is the X-ray of this patient. It looks like he has a cloud in his chest. And here you can see a round mark. That is the edge of a hole. There is a hole there where his lung has rotted away. He has it pretty bad in one lung, but the other one looks pretty good still.

"Was he living in the same hogan with you? How many other people were in that hogan? Did he ever go any place else? Do other people sometimes use his bedding and his dishes? The reason I am asking you all these questions is, when a boy has holes in his lungs from tuberculosis he can give it to another person pretty easy. Another person can catch it from him. You see, the lung that rotted and left that hole, he coughed that up in his spit, little at a time. That rotten lung has a lot of little tiny bugs or worms in it, so small that you can't see them. Maybe his spit got on his bedding or on his dishes. If somebody used the bedding or the dishes, maybe they got some of that spit into their lungs. That is the way a person can catch tuberculosis from a man who has it.

"Tuberculosis is a pretty bad disease. White people used to get it all the time, too, just like the Navahos, and they used to die from it all the time. Then they found out that to get well from tuberculosis a person has to take a long rest. He has to rest so much that he doesn't even sit up, he doesn't do any walking, he just lies there and helps his body to close up that hole by taking it easy. Besides resting he needs a lot of the right kind of food. He needs a lot of milk and eggs and meat and fruit. You know a person gets very poor (thin) when he has tuberculosis, and so we have to make him get fat again. White people found that if a person did all that resting and ate all that food, after a good many months he could begin to sit up, a few weeks more he could begin to walk a little, in a few months he could do a little easy work. Maybe in about two years he could go home and go back to work again. They found out if he didn't do all this resting, those holes in his lungs would get bigger and bigger, pretty soon no lungs left, can't breathe any more and he is dead.

"They found out that a hospital is the best place for a person with tuberculosis. It is hard to do all that resting at home, and it is hard to buy milk and fruit, and the other people there might catch his sickness. After he does all that resting and gets nice and fat there is not much chance that they will catch it.

"They found out that if you can start a person with tuberculosis to resting before he gets any holes in his lungs, he will get well quicker than if he already has some holes. If he only has a little bit of tuberculosis he will get well very soon if he takes a rest. You ought to bring to this hospital every person who has been in the hogan with this boy so we can take X-rays and see if any of them have caught tuberculosis from him. Then if they have we can get them well quicker than we can this boy. Maybe they can get well pretty soon."

sand painting
photo

A Sacred Sandpainting, Made of Multi-colored Sands and Ground Rock

Both Navaho and White Religious Leaders Took Part in the
Dedication of the Fort Defiance Hospital

HYPODERMOCLYSIS. "You have seen that this child can't drink anything. Every time she drinks she vomits it right up again. See how wrinkled her skin is getting? And see how dry her mouth is? Doctors have found out how to give a child like this a drink of water and the medicine she needs without her having to swallow it. It hurts the child a little bit, but if we don't do it she will probably get too dry and die because she can't drink. You don't want that to happen, do you? She is very sick, but I think she will be better and will feel better if we give her some water and some medicine. We have to put some hollow needles under her skin and let the water and medicine run in a little at a time. It will make a little swelling and will hurt a little, but that is not so bad as dying."

APPENDICITIS. "This woman has some pus in her guts one place. That is what makes it hurt in her side there. You know how it hurts when you get a boil on your skin? Well, this is like a boil, only it is in her guts. If we leave her alone, don't do anything, that pus will get more and more, maybe fill her whole belly, and she will get more and more sick until she dies. The best thing to do for that kind of sickness is to let her smell ether till it puts her to sleep. Then we make a little cut right where that pain is and find the place in her guts where there is some pus. We cut out that pus and sew up her guts and her side and then let her wake up. It doesn't hurt her at all because she is asleep all the time. After that she has to stay in the hospital ten days, and then you people can come and take her home. You see it isn't a very bad sickness if we operate on her right now, but if you put it off, don't let us operate for a few days, maybe by that time she will have too much pus in her belly, hard to cure, keep her sick a long time, maybe four weeks instead of only ten days. Maybe even the pus will get so much that it will be too strong. It will kill her even if we try to take it out if you let her wait too long."

TONSILLECTOMY. "I asked you people to come to see me because I want to talk to you about your little boy here. He has been in school here all winter, and all winter I have been taking care of him because he was sick so much. Most all the time he had a cold, and then lots of times he had a bad sore throat. Your little girl here, who was in school, too, I didn't hardly see her at all. She was pretty healthy all winter. I want you to look at her throat. See, it looks nice and even, no big lumps anywhere, no bright red anywhere. Now look at this boy's throat. Do you see those two big lumps back there? We call those lumps his tonsils. Last winter when he had those colds and those sore throats those two lumps swelled way up. They got real red, and there were some white places on them where there was some pus. Those two lumps hurt him a whole lot when they swelled up. Some times it looks as if he had a hard time to breathe with those two lumps there.

"White doctors have found out that when a boy's tonsils get like that, swell up pretty easy, get red, lots of colds and sore throats, that means there is a lot of sickness in those tonsils. They found out the best thing to do is to take out those tonsils. If they do that the boy won't have any sore throats, not so many colds. If they didn't do that, maybe after a while that sickness gets all through the boy's body, makes him very sick.

"We don't like to take them out when the boy's throat is sore or he has a cold. That makes it too hard on the boy. We like to wait till it gets warm weather like now and he doesn't have any cold or sore throat, and then take them out. We put him to sleep so that he doesn't feel it when we take those tonsils out. When he wakes up it will be a little sore in his throat. But in a few days' time, maybe four days, his throat will feel a whole lot better. Four more days, he will forget he had his tonsils out, and next winter he won't have any more sore throats and not so many colds.

"So I want to talk to you people about that because I know you like to have your boy nice and strong, and not have sore throats like he did this winter, and I hope you will ask me to take out his tonsils. If you make up your mind you want me to do that, you can leave the boy in the hospital right now and I will do it pretty soon. In that way you won't have to make another trip to bring the boy back to the hospital, and we can do it before he catches another cold."

OTITIS MEDIA. "The reason this little baby is crying all the time and holding onto her ear is that she has a lot of pus in her ear, and it hurts her a whole lot. It is like a boil, only it is way inside her ear. You can't even see it unless you look with something like this thing. I don't think I will show you what it looks like because it hurts the baby too much. You know, when you get a boil, the boil gets bigger and bigger, and pretty soon it breaks and a lot of pus comes out. Well, that is what will happen with this little baby if we don't help her. Only in the ear it is kind of small, and sometimes that pus breaks into the bone instead of outside, and then the bone here back of her ear would get all rotten and she would be very, very sick. The best thing to do for this baby is to open that place where the pus is with a little tiny knife so that the pus will run outside and not into the bone. In that way she will be all right in a few days.

"Do you nurse this baby? Well then, I think you and the baby had better stay in the hospital. That way the nurses can take care of the baby so her ear will get well pretty fast, and you can see how they do it and see that the baby is all right, too. It will be better for the baby if you come with her so that she will get the same food that she is used to. In that way I don't think you will have to stay very long, maybe twice four days."

SYPHILIS. The patient was a forty-five-year-old woman who came into the hospital for a broken wrist, suffered when she fell off a horse. Routine Wassermann found to be positive. No symptoms or other findings of syphilis.

"You remember we took some blood out of your arm the other day? We tested that blood and we found out you have a sickness you didn't know about. There is something wrong with your blood. Did you ever hear about anything like that in the Navaho way?

"I have heard that in the Navaho way if your father or mother does something like kill a snake or go to a ceremonial before you are born, maybe after many years you will get· sick from that. Is that true? Is there any way you can keep from getting sick if you know about that? (Right ceremonial.) Well, this disease you have in your blood is a little bit like that. Maybe you got it many years ago, but you didn't know anything about it. So far, it didn't make you sick. But maybe in a few more years it will make you very sick, maybe it will make your heart too big, or it will make your mind not work right.

"In the white way we can give you some medicine so you will never get sick from this thing, just like in the Navaho way you would have a ceremonial if your father had killed a snake. It is strong medicine and you can only take a little at a time, and you have to take it for one year. We have to put it in your arm or in your meat (muscle), and you will have to come to ―――― hospital every week for one year. If you do this you will never have any trouble with it, but if you don't keep coming every week for one year, maybe in a few years' time your heart will be too big or your mind will not work right. If you wait till you are sick in this way, it will be too late, this medicine will not cure you then, but if you take this medicine now, as I have been telling you, you will never get sick from this disease."

NAVAHO WAYS AND WHITE MAN'S
MEDICINE—IN OUT-PATIENT WORK

As WITH OURSELVES, so with the Navaho, the time will probably never come when everybody who gets ill is immediately hospitalized. There is little point in working toward such an end, but there are great possibilities for improving the way in which the sick are handled at home, both for their benefit and for the good of others.

In addition to using the suggestions for getting hygienic ideas across in a way familiar to the Navahos, any doctor, nurse or teacher working with the health problems has to realize the limitations imposed by the living conditions. Many things which we think of as simple necessities, like running water, beds and bedding, and screens, are either nonexistent for the Navahos or are in the luxury class. For instance their only running water would be that in the irrigation ditches or rivers. Some families live within a mile of a good spring or well; most of them have to go several miles to get a few gallons of water that may be full of silt. Gargling or using hot compresses under these circumstances can be recommended only with discretion. Again, the real necessity of bed rest should be carefully weighed. A man lying down in the daytime is a lazy man in the opinion of the Navahos; he has only a couple of sheepskins on the

dusty, draughty floor for a bed; he is in the way of the others; and
some one else is having to do his work. In some families, on the
other hand, a sick man can have a hogan to himself, which would
make staying on his back more feasible.

Patient, painstaking, and vivid explanations pay dividends in
hospital work, in the out-patient clinic at the hospital, and in the
day school. The same attitudes and customs have to be taken into
account, and the same pre-existing Navaho medical concepts can be
used to build upon. It is here, perhaps, that their custom of observ-
ing very precise and unvarying rules for their ceremonial treatment
of the sick will be of the greatest help, and it is here that you can
expect to do the most in diffusing modern ideas of hygiene and
public health.

In using any of these ideas, you will not succeed if you say to
your patient, "You believe you have to gather your plant medicine
just right and use it just the way the medicine man tells you, don't
you? Well, you ought to do the same thing with this medicine I
am giving you." This will sound to the Navaho as if some one had
been telling tales out of school, and he will resent the white man
ordering him to do something he knows much more about himself. It is more likely to be successful if used as questions, somewhat
as follows: "I hear in the Navaho way you have some good medicine. Is that true?" "Do you have some strong ones?" "How do you
get the strong ones?" Here you will probably be told that the
medicine man tells one of the men to go get them during a ceremonial, and you may even be told the exact way in which it is
done. "How do you use them?" "Well, in the American way we
have some strong medicines, too. This one (if it is digitalis, for instance) comes from a plant that grows in some parts of this country.
We pick the leaves and dry them and grind them up and then
press the powder very hard into these little pills. It makes a very
strong medicine, and too much of it will hurt a person. You have
to take it just the way I tell you, and then it will do your body lots
of good and make you strong again." The thing to keep in mind
is that the Navaho knows something as well as the doctor, and if
the doctor pays him the compliment of inquiring about it in an

Pine-clad Navaho Mountain

Pinyon and Cedar Country

interested way, he will not only learn a good deal about Navahos and their point of view, but he will enlist the loyalty and confidence of his patient, who will then do his utmost to follow instructions. If the doctor contents himself with handing an anemic patient a box of iron pills and telling him to take eight a day, he is less likely to be obeyed than if he makes it a point to explain that the tests he has made show that the patient's blood is not so red as it ought to be, it is a little weak, and it will be stronger if he can make it more red again. "These pills have some good medicine in them that will do that. Part of it is iron, but of course you can't eat iron, like the blade of your knife, just by itself. It wouldn't stay in your body but would go right through you. It is the same as when a woman wants to dye some wool: she uses one plant for the color, and another plant or some ashes or some ground-up rock to make the color stick to the wool. So this medicine has something else mixed with the iron to make it stay in your body. In the white way we believe that iron will make a man's body strong, but it will take four months to make your blood just right. You must take these pills just the way I tell you and then you will start to feel a little better pretty soon. You must take two of them in the morning when you can first see the sun; two more when the sun stands here (indicate position for ten o'clock in the morning); two more when the sun is here (indicate position for two o'clock in the afternoon); and two more at sundown. That makes four times every day. If you take it in that way and don't do too much hard work, you will get strong pretty fast. If you have to go away from your hogan you should carry some pills with you, so that you can take them at the right time. The pills I have given you will last for four weeks, one month. When they are almost gone you should come back and I will make another test to see how red your blood is getting and give you some more pills."

Even white patients would follow instructions better if they were more specific, but with the Navahos it is a matter of having respect for the medicine or not having it according to the importance the doctor seems to attach to it as judged by the care of his prescription.

Although the Navahos do not have many clocks and watches, the sun is a very reliable timekeeper and is used by them to estimate midmorning, noon, and midafternoon. First brightness in the east, sunup, and sunset are other well established points. To indicate time, one faces south, so that he faces the sun's path. With the right forefinger curled in a semicircle he will indicate the sun's position at the hour he is talking about.

Here follow some beliefs and customs that will appear more in dispensary practice than with patients in hospital and some concepts which are more useful in this connection than when nurses and hospital attendants have charge of cleanliness and decontamination techniques.

The Navahos have a deep-rooted fear of the dead. This is in part a fear of the ghost and in part a fear that by being near the dead they will come under the same evil supernatural influences that caused the death. This idea is very close to being afraid of the illness that caused the death. After a death Navahos usually get a white man to bury the corpse, but if they do it themselves a few persons are delegated for the purpose and they take off most of their clothing, avoid handling the body more than necessary, and fix up the hogan in which the death took place in such a way that no one will use it again. After the rites are over, they go through a long series of purification ceremonies, including bathing, and they avoid contact with others for four days. A hogan is often abandoned after serious illness even if death does not occur in it. A little understanding of their burial customs tends to make one more sympathetic with their habit of asking the nearest white man to bury their dead, or taking the patients to the hospital instead of letting them die at home. It is so much easier for a white man than for a Navaho.

Contagious illness could be described to Navahos as a state which is partly under the evil influences that cause death, and should be treated with similar isolation, including delegating certain members of the family to care for the patient, keeping the dishes separate, washing carefully, and maintaining a period of quarantine after the symptoms subside. One must be careful not to seem too cautious, however, or it may lead to desertion of the patient.

Portions of the body, such as hair-combings, nail parings, feces, urine, and saliva, are thought to be strongly associated with the life of the person of whom they were a part. Witches are able to bring harm to people by collecting such intimate castoffs of the body and doing evil things to them which soon affect the person from whom they came. Medicine men, endowed with the power of the gods, frequently use their saliva to help the patient by chewing and spitting concoctions on him. We would call most of these ideas magical, but it is a contagious magic and here we meet on common ground with the Navaho. We and they agree that saliva and excreta are important and powerful in some instances. Starting on such a basis, a doctor or nurse could draw parallels to show that the saliva and excreta of the sick are dangerous because they carry with them some of the evil that affects the sick person.

In making recommendations, one must remember that the less he interferes with the established way of life, the more successful he will be. One of the day school teachers was offended by the Navaho custom of spitting freely and forbade it inside her school. However, it was impossible to suppress the habit entirely, so she allowed spitting into tin cans partly filled with sand. During a subsequent measles epidemic she was pleased to find that in nearly every hogan where there were sick people, the patient was doing all his spitting into such a can or into a pile of soft sand which could be carried out on a shovel.

Fire is powerful. As lightning it may be full of danger or, if properly handled, will protect a person from other danger. As the means of heating the hogan and cooking food it is revered, and ceremonially it is one of the means taken to get rid of evil. From this start it is possible to recommend fire as a means of sterilizing things used by a sick person—burning the contents of sputum container, burning cloths used where there is pus, boiling or heating in the flame eating utensils the patient has used, and boiling his clothes and bedding when he recovers. When Navahos come to the hospital they may be shown the way the hospital sterilizes all contaminated objects and how the dishes are washed.

In some ceremonials (for example, the Chiricahua Apache Wind

Way) special food is cooked for the patient. What he does not eat must be destroyed, as it will cause sickness in any one else who eats it. This principle might be spread to all food a patient eats.

These remarks about contagion are suggestions about where to begin. The ultimate goal, of course, is to have Navahos thoroughly understand the nature of bacteria and other infecting organisms, and their control. To grasp this, however, a Navaho must have a high general level of education and acculturation, while any Navaho of normal intelligence can understand contagion as a spreading of evil influences and will be interested in hearing some new rules about it. A start could be made by preparing stained slides and showing them to the patient and his family whenever the case warranted it, as from tuberculous sputum or gonorrhoeal pus.

To show possible ways of giving directions for home treatment, the following descriptions are added:

MEASLES. A child of eight is brought to the doctor at the day school. He has a rash and Koplik spots, but shows no evidence of complications in ears, lungs, or kidneys. The doctor says:

"Has your little boy been around where there were some sick children? Well, I think he has caught the measles from some of them. Have you heard about measles? A lot of people are catching measles now. Do you have some other children? Are any of them sick? Have any of them had measles already?

"This boy is not very sick now, and if you do what I tell you he will probably get along all right. If you don't he might get pus in his ears, or in his lungs, or his kidneys might start to bleed.

"The first thing you have to do is to make him lie down all the time. That might be hard to do, but you must do it if you do not want him to get more sick. Keep him warm, but not so hot that he sweats. Four times a day he has to drink four cups of water—at sunup, and here (ten o'clock in the morning) and here (two in the afternoon) and at sundown, he must drink four cups of water. He can eat some of the food you eat if you cook it nice and soft for him. Make him some soup, and cook him some rice and potatoes in the soup.

A Sandstone "Monument"

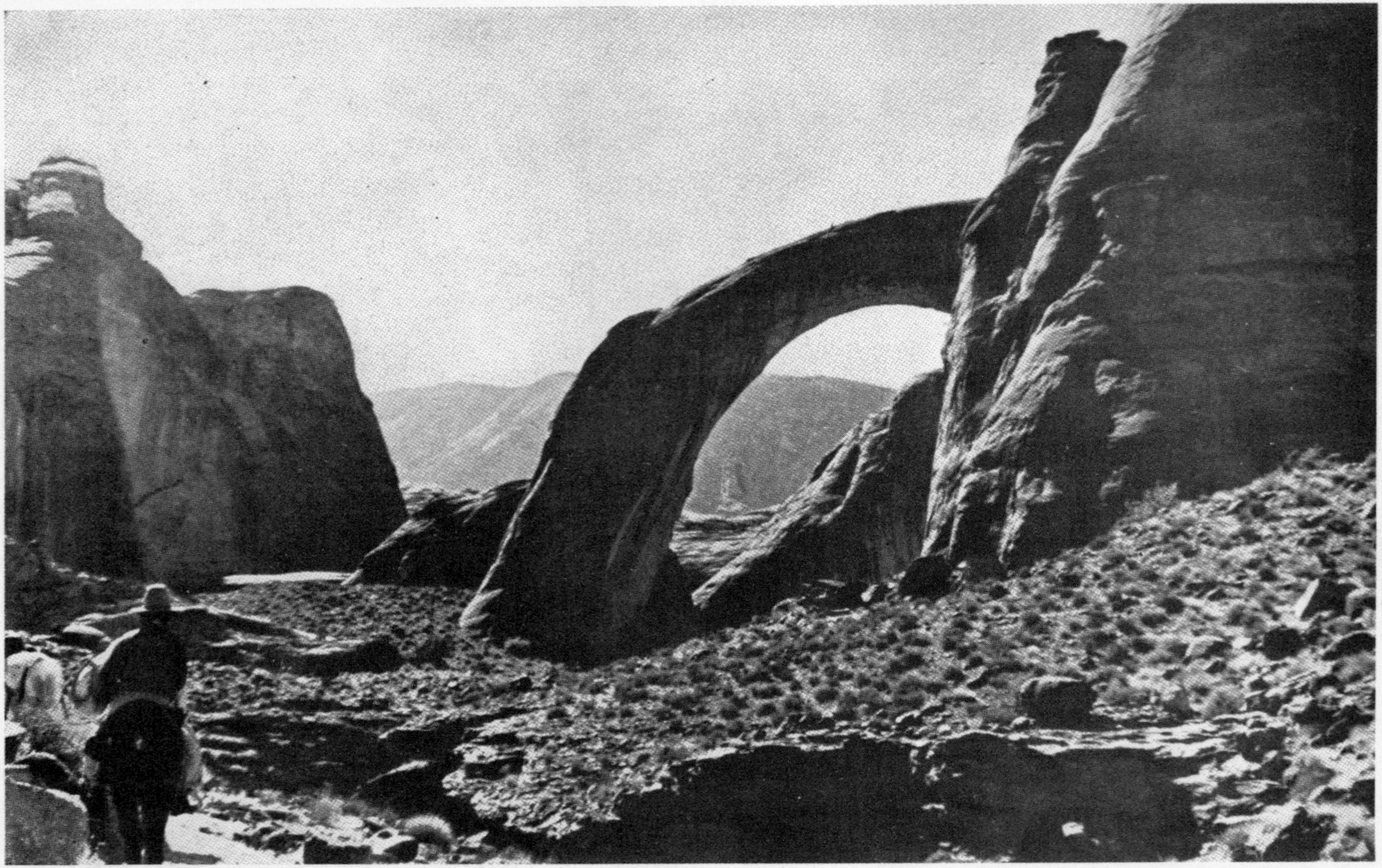

Photograph by the authors

"Get him something to play with so he won't mind so much having to stay in bed. Keep him in bed all the time for four days, and then for four days more. When he has to go to the toilet, carry him out on a blanket or let him do it in a pile of sand on a shovel that you can take outside. If he spits, make him do it in a can with some sand in it. After eight days he can begin to sit up, and in four days more you can let him walk outside a little.

"You must keep the other children away from him as much as you can, but if they begin to get sick, you can put them to bed alongside this boy and take care of them the same way I have been telling you.

"Don't let any other children come to play with your children because if they do they will get the measles, too. Don't let them go to Sings or to the traders. Just keep them at home, but if they get the measles, take good care of them and they won't get too sick either."

IMPETIGO. A child of two is brought in with a good many crusts on his face, which is smeared with red clay and grease. He has had the crusts for one week and his mother has one on her breast. The doctor says:

"This child has some skin disease, and you have caught it from him a little, on your breast. We have some ointment here that is good for that kind of skin disease. This ointment is made with the grease from sheep's wool and some special kind of white rock that they grind up real fine. When they put the ground-up rock in the grease, that makes it all soft and it helps this kind of skin disease a whole lot. You will have to use it just the way I tell you or it won't do much good.

"The baby is not going to like what you have to do to cure this skin trouble, but you will have to let him cry a little. There are some very, very small bugs underneath these crusts. This ointment here will kill those bugs, but the crusts make it too safe for them. You have to take off the crusts first, and then the ointment will kill the bugs.

"I will let you do it because the baby knows you and you can do it kind of easy. First let's wash off this grease and clay with this liquid soap. Now let's pull off these crusts, kind of gently, but quick, and then it won't hurt the baby so much. Now take some of this ointment and rub it into his face pretty good. Don't let him scratch his face any because that will just make it more sore. Now do the same thing to that place on your breast. That is very good. You are almost like a nurse.

"I will give you some of this ointment and a bottle of this liquid soap to take home with you, and some of this cloth to use to wash his face. I want you to use it this way: In the morning at sunup do just like you did now, wash his face, take off the crusts, rub in the ointment. When the sun is here (ten o'clock) rub in some more ointment. When the sun is here (two o'clock) rub in some more ointment. At sundown wash his face, take off the crusts, rub in some more ointment. Can you remember everything that I told you?

"Do you have some other children? Don't let them touch the baby till his face is all cured, or they may get some sores, too. And don't let them use this cloth. Keep the cloth just to wash his face and your breast. Every morning after you have washed his face with it you ought to put it in an old pot with some water and let it boil in the fire quite a while. Then hang it out in the sunshine. The boiling water and the sunshine will kill any of the bugs that get on the cloth from under the crusts. Don't use the pot for anything else, and when his face is all well, throw the pot and the cloth away. Do all these things just like I have told you and his face will get better pretty quick."

MALNUTRITION. A mother brings in a baby of nine months with complaint that he is not very fat and he cries all the time. The doctor says:

"What do you feed this baby? He just sucks? Do you give him anything else to eat? Not anything? Well, I think maybe you do not have enough milk for this baby. Did you ever hear about mothers who don't have enough milk? I have seen some mothers who don't have any milk at all, and I have seen lots of them who don't have enough for their babies when they get as old as this boy.

Is he your first baby? I guess that is why you didn't hear about that yet. I think this baby is not getting enough to eat, he is hungry. Does he cry a lot? Well, that is because he is hungry. What kind of food do you eat? Bread, coffee and mutton? I think that is too strong for this baby yet. He doesn't have many teeth to chew that mutton or that bread with, does he? He can't swallow that kind of food very well if he doesn't chew it up first.

"Maybe you can do this: Maybe you can get some milk for him. Do you know anybody who has some goats? You have some goats? Well, that is fine. Do you milk them? No? Do they look like they had some milk? Well, I think this boy needs two cups of goat's milk every day, two full cups. Do you think you can get that much? He doesn't want it all at one time. He can have half a cup of goat's milk four times every day. Does he drink water out of a cup? Oh, he never drinks any water? Well, you can see if he will drink the goat's milk out of a cup. If he doesn't like that, you can buy him a bottle and a nipple at the traders. If you buy him a bottle and nipple, you have to keep them nice and clean. Every time he has a drink of goat's milk, right after that you have to wash the bottle and the nipple with hot water and put it where the flies won't walk on it. Every morning you have to put that bottle and nipple into some water in a pot and put it in the fire until it boils hard. That way you can keep it nice and clean.

"I want you to give this baby one-half cup of goat's milk when you can just see the sun; then one-half cup more when the sun is right here (ten o'clock); then one-half cup more when the sun is here (two o'clock); and then one-half cup at sundown. Can you remember what I told you?

"Do you eat any mutton in your home? You have it every week? Well, if you make some soup for this baby, he can eat that. You can put it in his mouth with a spoon. Don't let it be too hot. And do you have some potatoes? He can have some potatoes if you cook them nice and soft and mash them up for him.

"If you give him all that to eat, I think he will get nice and fat, and I don't think he will be crying much. Bring him back here in four weeks and we will see how fat he is getting."

BUGS IN HAIR. The complaint is that a little girl of seven has sores in her hair. Her hair is matted and full of nits. The sores are excoriations from scratching bug bites. The doctor says:

"It looks to me like this little girl has lots of bugs in her hair. They make her head itch, and when she scratches she pulls the skin right off and makes a sore place. When did you wash her hair last time? Long time ago? I am sorry you didn't wash it every week. If you wash it every week with yucca and lots of water, it wouldn't have so many bugs in it.

"Now she has so many bugs it is kind of hard to get rid of them. Shall we cut all her hair off? It will grow again pretty soon. You don't want to do that? Then I will tell you what you have to do to get rid of these bugs. First take this comb and comb her hair good. That is going to take you quite a while. ———— Is it all combed? That looks a lot better already. You ought to comb her hair every day if she can't do it herself. Now come over here and wash it for her in this basin with this yellow soap. Yucca root would be good to wash it with, but I don't have any yucca. Get a lot of soap into it, and then rinse it all out so there isn't any soap left. There, that looks good. I think most of the bugs are killed now, but you see all these little white things in her hair? Those are kind of like seeds. A new bug comes out of every one of those white things unless you get rid of them or kill them.

"Now here is some kerosene. That is the same stuff you put in lamps to make a light. This will get into those little white seeds and kill them. You don't have to use a whole lot. Just sprinkle a little on her hair. Try not to get it into the sore places or it will make them sting. Put it on the hair in back too, the long hair. Now we have to put her hair up on top of her head and tie some cloth around it so that kerosene will stay there a while and won't dry up too fast. That is good. Now leave it there till sundown. Tonight she can take that cloth off and let her hair loose.

"You have to do these things I showed you for the next four days. Every day right after breakfast do all these things, and then leave that cloth on her head till sundown.

"Do some of your other children have bugs? Not so bad as this girl? Well, I think you ought to do all these things to their hair, too, to get rid of the bugs. You ought to try to find out where the bugs come from. Maybe there are a lot of them in the sheepskins or in the blankets. If you find a lot in the blankets, wash them in real hot water and hang them in the sunshine to dry. If there are a lot in the sheepskins, try to get rid of those sheepskins and get some new ones.

"Don't forget after you get rid of all the bugs to wash all the children's hair every week with yucca and water. That way you won't have any more trouble with them, I think."

A SPEECH ON HEALTH

WE HAVE POINTED OUT BEFORE that one important function of the doctor is that of health-educator. Numerous occasions present themselves at which it would be suitable to talk to the Navahos about health and hygiene. The following speech has been prepared as a sample for such use. It may be that in the particular area where a doctor is working, the problems mentioned may not be as important as some others, or it may seem that too much is included for a single speech. It is not intended to be used as it stands, but to serve as a pattern and to suggest possibilities for getting our medical concepts over to the Indians in understandable language.

As with the other examples given, the expressions used are those of the interpreter with whom the writers are most familiar. They might have to be changed to a large extent with different interpreters.

"It sure is nice to see so many of you people here today. I know some of you live a long way from here and it takes a long time to come here, so I sure appreciate it that you came to hear me talk. I had to come a long way, too, —— miles, to talk to you people.

Today the road was pretty good so I could come pretty easy. If the road was muddy maybe I wouldn't be here yet.

"It is pretty hard for you people to come to the doctor, or for the doctor to come to you when the roads are bad. Even trucks can't get through sometimes. That makes it bad when some one gets sick. I know sometimes you can't even get to the telephone to call for the ambulance, and sometimes the ambulance is busy going off some other place when you call. Then sometimes we send the ambulance away out many miles, and maybe we can't find the right family, or maybe they have changed their minds when we get there and don't want to go to the hospital. That makes it hard for us, too. Maybe while the ambulance is trying to find that family, or the driver is trying to tell the patient to come to the hospital, somebody else way out south of here calls for the ambulance. Then that sick person has to wait a long time before the ambulance can come for him.

"Well, in this way, you can see it is hard for both sides—it is hard for the hospital and it is hard for you people who get sick. So I want to tell you today a little about how to keep from getting sick.

"Maybe some of you older people remember the time many years ago when there was a bad disease that we call smallpox going around among the Indians. People who caught that sickness got big sores all over the body and a lot of them died pretty fast. The ones that didn't die, when they got better they had lots of little marks all over the body where the sores had been, and you can still see those marks today.

"At that time white people had a lot of that sickness, too, and a lot of them died from it. Even the white people's cows got a disease just about like smallpox, only not quite so bad, and they didn't die from it. They would just get a little sick with it. Looks like they were stronger than the people. Then the white doctors found out that if they took a little bit of pus from one of those cows that were just a little sick and put it on a person's arm and made just a little sore place there, that person will never get that bad sickness. That is what we call vaccination, and nowadays we try to do that for everybody, both white people and Indians. You can see the mark where that little sore was on my arm, and you can see it on the arm of the schoolboys and girls and anybody else who was vaccinated. We will never get the smallpox if we have it done every four years, and even one time helps a whole lot.

"It is the same way with that kind of bad sore throat that we call diphtheria. Just a few years ago a lot of Navahos began to get that bad sore throat. Well, the white doctors had already found out what to do for it because the white people had that sickness, too. For the people who already had that sickness, they gave them some very strong medicine in their meat (muscle) down here. This kind of medicine comes from the blood of a horse that is so strong he never gets this kind of sore throat. They take some of the horse's blood and they pour it through cloth some way so that only the watery part comes through, and they use that watery part. They can't use every horse for this, only special ones. If the people hadn't been sick too long, that medicine would kill the sickness that was in their throats and they would get better. Sometimes it was too late and the medicine couldn't cure them. At that time, too, the doctors used a little bit of that kind of medicine for the people who didn't have the sore throat yet. They put it into the meat (muscle) on their arm, and those people never did catch the bad sore throat after that.

"It is the same way with a few other sicknesses. White doctors have found out some kind of medicine to give for each different sickness so that a person will never get that kind of sickness. I am sorry to say that there are still some kinds of sickness like tuberculosis that we don't have any medicine to keep people from getting it. White doctors in the big hospitals in the east and in the west are working all the time to try to find some more of those medicines, but so far they haven't found any for tuberculosis.

"With white children we give all of them the medicine to keep them from getting all those sores and that bad sore throat, and we are trying to do the same thing for Navaho children. There are a lot of you older people who haven't had those two kinds of medicine, and I hope you will tell me and let me give it to you. I have it right here with me, so you people and I won't have to make another long trip for that. As soon as I finish talking I will do that for you people.

"There is another thing I want to tell you about so you can keep from getting sicknesses. I think you have, every one of you, seen some people who caught measles when measles was going around just a little while ago. I guess you could see how one child would maybe go to the traders and see some one there who had measles, and after he came home, in about ten days, he would begin to feel a little sick, like he had a little cold. Then pretty soon he has some spots on his skin, and in his mouth, and the next day he has a rash all over. Then in about ten days the other children and maybe some of the older people get that same kind of trouble. It is the same way with that disease called smallpox, and that diphtheria that I was telling you about before. If a person goes where there is some one with that kind of sickness, most likely he will catch it. It is the same way with TB and flu, and colds. Some kinds of trouble are not catching. If you go where a man has a broken leg, you won't get a broken leg, too. You all know that, I am sure.

"I heard that in the days when the Navahos had the smallpox they had a good way to keep from catching it from each other. If they saw that one person in the family was getting it, they built him a brush hogan, or maybe the rest of the family moved into a brush hogan and left him by himself. One other person in the family took care of the sick one. They cooked his food and put it outside the door and the one who was taking care came to get it. They never got close to this one who was taking care, either. They would just call to her and ask how the sick one was getting along and tell her the news. That way there was only one sick one in the family instead of all the family getting smallpox.

"I have heard some other things about how you treat sickness in the Navaho way. Maybe it is the truth, maybe not. You people know more about that than I do. I have heard that in the Navaho way you have some Sings, where you cook different pieces of a sheep for the patient. If the patient doesn't eat it all, you have to throw the rest away because some one else who eats it will get sick from that Sing. Did I hear that in the right way? Well, I think that is a good thing. In the white way, too, we believe that nobody should eat food left over from a sick person. We believe that a little bit of his sickness can get into that food and if somebody else eats that food maybe that person will get sick, too.

"I have heard also that in the Navaho way after a person has a Sing, for four days after that, he stays quiet and keeps by himself and doesn't do any work, and eats by himself. Did I hear that in the right way? Well, I think that is good, too. That is what we do in the white way. After a person has been sick, even when he begins to feel better, we still keep him quiet for a few days, and keep him away from other people. We do that because we believe that after a person has been sick he needs to rest for a while, and we also believe that even when he begins to feel better maybe he can still give his sickness to someone else if he mixes with other people.

"Now I think it would help you out a whole lot if you do these same things when you find out someone in your family has TB. You remember I just told you that the white doctors haven't found any medicine yet that will keep a person from getting TB. And they haven't found any medicine that will kill the TB bugs right away, either. I am sorry to have to say these things, and I sure hope that pretty soon they will be able to find the right medicine, but so far they haven't done it. I guess you know that TB is one of the worst diseases for Navahos right now. Most all of you people know someone who died of TB. Maybe a lot of you have someone in your family who has TB right now.

"A few years ago it was that same way with the white people. Almost every family had someone with TB, and lots of people died with TB. Then the white doctors worked very hard to try to get rid of TB, and they found out a lot of things about it. They found out that TB is catching, just like smallpox and that bad sore throat (diphtheria) that I was telling you about. Only it takes longer for a person to know he has TB. He doesn't have any sore on his body, and he doesn't get sore throat. Maybe if he did he would go to the doctor for some treatment quicker. TB comes on kind of slowly, and sometimes you don't know you have it till one day you cough real hard and some blood comes up in your spit. There is one way the white doctors found out they could tell when a person had TB real early, and that is X-ray. With X-ray they can take a picture of your lungs, and they can see right off if you have TB or if your lungs are all right.

"I brought some pictures with me today for you people to see. Here is one of a person with good lungs. See how nice and even they look? Just the same on both sides. This thing here is the windpipe you breathe with, and here is this man's heart, but it is his lungs we are interested in. Now here is a person just beginning to get TB. See, there is this little cloudy place right here? One side is all nice and even, but the other side has this little TB in it. This man came to the hospital and let us take care of him and it didn't take him very long to get well again. Here is another picture of a person with TB. This person has more TB than the other one. See, there is a bigger cloud in his chest, and here you can see a round thing. That round thing is a hole where the TB has rotted his lung away. That person would be coughing and spitting a lot, and every time he coughs some of the TB bugs come up in his spit. If he stays at home and spits on the floor, maybe it gets on the sheepskins and blankets, and then other people get it into their lungs, and pretty soon they have the TB, too. Or maybe the children play on the floor where that spit is, and they get it on their hands, and then they put their hands into their mouths, and pretty soon they have TB. Children can get TB pretty easy in that way. Of course, if that person is careful to spit into a tin can with some sand in it, and not to get any spit on anything that other people use, then the others maybe won't get TB from that person. Or if he always spits into the fire so the fire burns the bugs up, that is better yet. Now I will show you one more X-ray. This person had TB for many years before he came to the hospital. You can see his whole lungs look pretty bad. You can see lots of holes in them, and there is hardly any place where there is not some TB. A man like this probably won't live very long. You can see he doesn't have hardly any lungs left to breathe with. Too bad he didn't come to the hospital many years ago when he first got TB. Then maybe he would be all right by this time.

"The white doctors learned that if a person finds out he has TB when it is like that first TB X-ray, if he takes care of himself in the right way, his body can kill off that TB pretty easy, maybe in about one year. If he doesn't find out till he has an X-ray like that second sick one, it takes a lot longer, maybe four years, for his body to kill off that TB. If he doesn't find out till his lungs look like that last picture, there is not much that his body can do, the TB is too strong for him to kill it by that time.

"I hope you listened good when I said the patient's *body* has to kill off that TB. That is because we haven't found any medicine to do that job yet. But there are a lot of things a person can do to help his body fight pretty strong. The white doctors found these things out with white people, and they are just as good for Navahos.

"The first thing a person with TB has to do is to give his body lots of rest. If he goes to the hospital they put him to bed. If he doesn't go to the hospital you ought to build him his own hogan so he can go to bed there, and there won't be a lot of people walking around him. If it is summer time you can build him a shade and just let him lie down out there all the time. Somebody ought to bring him his food just like the nurses do in the hospital, so that he doesn't have to get up and walk into the other hogan for that. You ought to fix it some way so he doesn't have to walk outside to go to the toilet. Maybe you can fix him a pile of sand that you can take outside for him after he uses it. Or you can carry him outside on a blanket. He ought to lie right down flat for a long time, maybe four months, not even sit up, not do any walking. At the end of that four months he can start to sit up a little bit. Maybe when he has been sitting up for four weeks, not doing any walking yet, you can take him to the hospital for an X-ray and for the doctor to see him, see how he is getting along. If he is getting along all right, maybe he can start to walk around a little bit, but not very much. He can't do any work yet, not for four months more. Then take him back to the doctor again.

"About his food: he needs to take a lot of food. He needs a lot of meat, and you ought to buy him some milk at the store to drink, and you ought to buy him oranges, and get him some cod-liver oil. If it is summer time let him eat lots of vegetables from your garden. If you have some goats you can get some milk from them for him.

"About his dishes: he ought to have his own dishes that no one else uses. If you can't do that, then every time he uses them, afterward you have to boil them in the fire for about half an hour. If you don't do that maybe someone in the family will catch his TB from those dishes. If there is any food left over on his dishes, you must throw it away or burn it up.

"About his bedding: no one else must use his sheepskins or his blankets. Every four days you ought to hang his sheepskins out in the sun for one whole day. And every four weeks you ought to wash his blanket and hang that in the sun all day. The sun can kill the TB poison pretty easy, and so can fire.

"About his spit: even if he is in a hogan by himself, you ought to make him spit into a tin can that has some sand in the bottom. Every day in the morning you ought to burn that spit and sand in a good fire, and put some clean sand in the can for him. In that way the fire will protect you and there won't be any poison spit lying around for anyone to catch TB from.

"Now those are a lot of things you have to do for a person who has TB. It is not very easy for you to do these things, and the person with TB doesn't always like to do them. But you have to do all these things just like I tell you if you want the person to get well from his TB, and if you don't want other people in your family to catch it.

"Of course, you can take him to the hospital if you want to, but sometimes the hospitals have too many sick people already, and they can't take him. And I have heard that sometimes you don't like to take a person with TB to a hospital because he has to stay there so long. If you do all the things I have told you, you can keep him home and take care of him in the right way and keep the other people safe, too.

"There is just one more thing I want to tell you about TB. Maybe you people will want to have a Sing for a person who has TB that you are taking care of at home. I have heard that there are a lot of different Sings in the Navaho way, some long ones and some short ones. In some of them the patient has to walk around a whole lot, and in others he doesn't have to walk around so much. I have heard that in most of them the patient has to sit up all night long. Now here is what I think: if you want to have a Sing, have one that will be kind of easy for the patient as long as he is doing all that resting. It would be better to wait for four months, until he is sitting up a little, and then have the Sing. Even then, try to have the medicine man let him lie down while he is doing the singing for the patient. I have heard that the ceremonial we call "Blessing Way" in English, and you call Hozhoonji in Navaho, is a very good Sing for anybody who is sick, and is not too hard on the patient. I know you people have to choose your own Sing, but I am just telling you what I think about it.

"Well, that is enough about TB, I think. Now, I would like to tell you a few other things about the way people can live to keep well and not get sick. A lot of these things you know about, and a lot of you do them. I know that some things are hard for you to do, like things that need a lot of water. Some of you live where there is good water pretty close, some of you have to go a long way to get water and then it is pretty dirty. I am sorry for you people who don't have much water. Maybe some time there will be more wells, and it will be better for you people. Right now you just have to get along the best way you can.

"The reason I talk about water is that doctors believe that if you keep your bodies and everything around you nice and clean, you won't get sick so much as if everything is dirty. I know that some of you people come here to the day school a whole lot and wash your clothes and wash your bodies. Other people don't come very much. Maybe they live too far away. It is a very good thing to come to wash like that. If you get dirty, then you can wash all the dirt off. If you get bugs on you, you can kill them off pretty good with soap and water, and you don't have to scratch so much. If some of you people live too far away from the day school to come here to wash, you can wash at home with yucca root and water. That is a good kind of bath. After you are all clean, put on some clean clothes and wash your dirty ones. That is a good way to get rid of bugs, too. If you don't have any good water to wash with, you can take a sweat bath. That gets you clean and makes you feel good, too. Everybody ought to take some kind of a bath every four days, and if you can do it any way, you ought to put on clean clothes every four days, too. If you put on dirty clothes, you get dirty right away; no use to take the bath. If you have bugs, they are in the clothes and when you put on the dirty clothes they jump right back onto you again and start to bite you. Another thing I notice a lot of you people do already that I think is very good, and that is that you wash your hands before you eat. In the white way we think that is very good, because if you eat with dirty hands, a lot of dirt gets into your mouth and maybe that will make you sick. So if there are any of you people who don't wash your hands before you eat, try to remember that and do that.

"One more thing about keeping clean, and that is keeping the babies clean. I know that some of you wash your babies every day, and you wash out the cloths you use to catch their water every day. I see that some others just let those cloths dry, they don't wash them, and they don't wash the babies very much. That way the babies smell pretty bad all the time, and sometimes they get pretty sore around the legs. I think the mothers who wash their babies and wash the cloths do the best thing. That keeps the babies from getting sick a whole lot. Of course, in the winter time you can't wash the babies if the hogan is cold, but you can get your hogan nice and warm and then wash the baby nice and quick and wrap him up again. In that way, it is a very good thing to do.

"Then there is something I want to say about spitting. I see that most of you people spit a whole lot. White people do it, too, but white people learned that they have to be careful where they spit. They learned that you have to spit so that the little tiny bugs that are in everybody's spit won't hurt other people. You remember what I said about spit from a person who has TB. Well, he has very strong bugs in his spit, but most anybody has some bugs, and especially children can get sick from the spit from older people.

You remember I told you that a person with TB ought to spit into a can with some sand in it, and every morning he ought to burn that spit and sand in the fire. Well, it would be a good thing if everybody who spits did that, but I know you can't do it all the time. There are some things everybody can do all the time. One thing is to spit in the fire if you are inside the hogan. That way the spit is where the children won't get it on their hands, and the fire will soon burn up the bugs that are in it so they won't hurt anybody. If there is no fire, spit outdoors where the sunshine is, and that way the sunshine will kill the bugs. You may not believe all that I am telling you, but it is what the white people have found out, and it has helped them to keep from getting sick.

"Well, I have told you a whole lot of things now. Maybe you have heard some of it before this, maybe some of it is new to you. I hope you will remember what I have told you and will try it out and see if it is good. Maybe you would like to ask me some questions now. I will try to answer them the best way I can.

"I sure appreciate that all you people came from so far to hear me talk today, and I hope that what I told you will help you out a whole lot. The white doctors that work with you people all want to see you getting stronger and stronger all the time, and learning how to help your own selves when you get sick, because it is so far to the hospital, and sometimes there are not enough doctors to take care of the people who get sick. If you know what to do when somebody gets sick, it will help you people and the doctors, too."

Similar chapters could doubtless be written from the point of view of an educator, or an economist, or an agriculturist. It is to be hoped that in future someone with training along those lines will treat those subjects, which the present authors do not feel equipped to handle. It is our opinion that similar methods would be effective in any relationship where technicians from white culture are trying to educate the Navahos in a new way of doing things.

An Especially Dry Spot on the Western Part of the Reservation

Navaho Timber Resources

U. S. Indian Service photograph

Recess at a Day School

Photograph by Helen M. Post

Mothers and Babies as well as Pupils Come to the Day School

U. S. Indian Service photograph

Other Users of a Day School

NAVAHO LIVES

THIS CHAPTER is devoted to life stories told us by the Navahos. They are presented in order to give some personal idea of how a Navaho views his life. All three people are middle-aged or over, which means that they have not been "educated." One of them spent a few years at school and his account will give some idea of what the Indian schools used to be like. The names of people and places have been changed so as to conceal their identity.

STORY I

This is an account of a Navaho man of about forty years who has lived outside the reservation. Part of it is in his own words, as interpreted by another Navaho, part is written by the authors in order to shorten the story and add material from other sources.

Jaime is a Navaho of medium height and athletic build with a shy but friendly manner. We first saw him in the late winter of 1940 when we were living with an Indian family at the edge of a pinyon forest in western New Mexico. He would stroll across the sun-warmed clearing under a black ten-gallon hat, trailing big-wheeled spurs, and often sat most of the day in the sun with his back against a wall, or shot marbles with one of the children. Sooner or later he would come into the house where we lived and sit for an hour or two, saying little but smiling much. After dark he would disappear in the woods, walking home under the moon, his pockets full of cigarettes which we had given him, at his suggestion.

When we inquired about him we were told that he lived with his wife and two children about three miles away, was hard working, poor, but an expert at practicing Hand-trembling. This, as you will remember, is a mystic and inspired method of diagnosing the cause of illness, finding lost articles, and pointing out witches. Several anecdotes were given us to illustrate his power.

After a little, when we had begun to take life stories from other Indians, Jaime came and offered to tell his story if we would come and stay with him for a while. We were glad to capitalize on this spontaneous offer.

Jaime was born about 1902 near the region where he now lives, and was the oldest of three brothers. When he was about seven his mother died and he became the charge of one of his maternal aunts and his maternal grandparents. His father took no part in his up-bringing.

Like most Navaho children, Jaime spent a good part of his time out herding the family's sheep. "One day I saw a man coming along with big white whiskers all over his face. The skin that showed was around his eyes, just a little bit. I had never seen a white man before. I ran away home and told the people I had seen something out there coming toward the sheep. It looked like a man, I said, but had wool all over its face. I thought the whiskers were wool, and I wasn't sure it was a man. Roberto, my grandfather, was sitting outside the hogan having coffee and Navaho bread. He said, 'That must have been a white man you seen.' Pretty soon the man came up, walked up to Roberto, reached under his vest and pulled out below the left arm a bunch of chili peppers. He peeled off three and gave them to Roberto, then he pointed to the bread and then down his throat. The women didn't want to feed him, but Roberto said, 'Give him some.' The pile of bread soon went away down. Then the white man stood up, pointed away to the west, and walked off that way. Next day some of the Indian boys trailed him to see which way he was going. They found where he had spent the night, dug a hole and lit a tiny fire and laid down by it all night. Then his tracks went on toward the west."

The family group was dominated by the grandfather, Old Man Roberto, one of the most distinguished Singers in the region. In spite of this religious atmosphere, Jaime was not encouraged to participate, but was told that his place was with the sheep until he was older. He was not "supposed to take care of ceremonials, but he was supposed to take care of sheep." He was supposed to "herd the sheep all the time, every day, and not go over to a ceremonial or any other place, only herding."

One day at the age of eleven, when he heard about a ceremonial being performed near by, he decided that he would like to see it, so he headed the sheep toward home and ran away. At first he was afraid to approach the hogan where the ceremonial was being held, and hid behind a hill. After dark he approached a little closer and was finally seen and brought inside. He was encouraged to join, and had some of what was going on explained to him.

"Everybody started singing, but I am not singing. I just sit there. The people told me, 'Why don't you sing? You must help sing, that is what we are here for, all of us, we come here for a ceremonial. You must have come here for something else.' When they started singing again I tried to sing, but I don't know what I was singing about, I just help holler, that is all. When they stopped singing they told me, 'That is right, sing, but sing louder yet.' We sing and they brought in food and we eat, and then we sing till daylight. There was a lot of food there to eat, and there was singing. I like to hear the song. And the corn pollen they had, all of that made me think pretty with the ceremonial."

As he got older he was allowed to see more of the ceremonial life. Between eleven and fifteen he saw at least six large ceremonials, and his interest in them grew. At first he was hurt when his grandfather refused to tell him what everything meant. "There is a lot of story there," the old man said, "but you don't need to know now.

You will find it out for yourself in a few years." He was told that the ceremonials and the religious beliefs were not made up by the Navahos, but were given them by the gods.

"I didn't quite believe what I had been told. I thought the ceremonials might be true, but I also thought they might not. Maybe they did some good and maybe not. After I saw my grandfather treat some patients and he told me that the Navahos didn't make up these songs but they were given by the Holy People, from there on I begin to believe little by little, more and more."

During his fourteenth year he watched one of his maternal uncles, Julio, learn part of a ceremonial from the grandfather. It was in the winter and Jaime was on hand to attend the fire. "My grandfather Roberto sang one song, Julio also sang. After they sang this song a few times, my grandfather told Julio try it out by himself. He sing. 'Wasn't right,' said Roberto. They stay with it and sing together till Julio can sing his song by himself. It takes about two hours. I bring the wood inside and build up the fire while he is doing this. They keep up this singing till way past midnight, then they let it go till next night. Roberto used to tell some old legends to Julio. I was just listening and watching. Some nights I went too sleepy. Every time I do that, they wake me up. They make me sit up and tend to the fire. While they doing this, I begin more believe it."

On being asked if he ever wished to become a Singer, he replied, "I never had time, I was always working, herding sheep, working for Mexican, working for white man, working for my own. Then it was a lot of work to remember all that, I was afraid to start it." Our interpreter added this comment to which Jaime gave assent, "These Singers, when they teach you, they don't let you sleep. You have to sit up straight. If you bend over, they say, 'Hey!' and make you sit up, and even if you get too sleepy they won't let you sleep, you got to keep going with it. Young people are afraid of that."

During these years the economic returns from being a Singer were not lost on Jaime, as he mentions from time to time in his account some of the pay his grandfather received.

Hand-trembling came to his attention at least as early as the other forms of religious practice. The atmosphere in which he lived was saturated with it. Four of the family, three maternal aunts and a maternal uncle, practiced it. When about nine he witnessed the first performance, done by one of his aunts. "My aunt got up and sit in right close to the patient. They gave her some water and she wash her hands. After she did that, she wants all the children to be sent out. Wanted to have just grown people there. She says that she don't want no noise when she starts this, tell the people outside not to come inside. She told the children stay away from this hogan, make no noise near the hogan. She sent somebody outside to watch for travellers, to stop them and not let them come inside till she was finished. She take the corn pollen and sprinkle it on her hand, sits on the northeast side of the patient, hold her hand out and sit there still. She sits there for quite a while like that, and then her hand begins to shake. It gets more shaking and more till she reach over on the patient, just kind of feel over his body, on the arm, hand, chest, and all over. While she did that, I watch in the face, and she close her eyes. After she quit, she is breathing pretty strong, seems like she running. After a little while the father of the patient asked her what she found out. She says that when the patient's mother was carrying the patient before he was born, the father killed a snake, chopped off its head. That give the patient a pretty strong pain inside the chest and on up to the throat. The father study this over to see whether he remember he did it or not. He says yes he did it when out herding one time. My aunt says the patient is pretty sick and they must hurry and do something about it. She think her father, my grandfather Roberto, could be the man that cure the patient."

This plan was carried out and Jaime watched his grandfather work for two days. At first the patient was so sick that he had to be carried in and out of the hogan on a blanket, but after two days he began to walk around by himself. The aunt received one big sheep and two big turquoise tied together, while the grandfather got five big sheep and some calico that had been provided by the sick man's family for use in the ceremonial. He gave some of the sheep meat and calico to Jaime.

Concerning his aunt's performance, Jaime said, "I think very hard about it. She did it there and I watch pretty close, and I couldn't see how she could tell all these things what is happen. I couldn't get that thing straight, so I can tell. I been thinking that I was going to ask one of the persons that do Hand-trembling, but some people told me that these Hand-trembling people are not allowed to tell anybody. Then I seen Hand-trembling some more after that. I found out by thinking is the best way to do it. It looks like some of these people who don't think hard enough to do Hand-trembling, they don't get it very straight. These kind of people never get the right Singer to cure a person. They think slowly about it and can't think hard enough. Sometimes they guess right, sometimes they only guess pretty close. I think this is the way it is."

When about fifteen he had an attack of Hand-trembling sickness. He was lying alone in the hogan, and he describes his experience thus: "I wasn't feeling very good. You know some days you act like you are going to sleep, want to lie down. I feel that way. I was lying down on the northeast side facing east toward the doorway and I went to sleep for a little while. When I woke up my legs and feet and whole body was feeling all large, just like when you sit down and your legs went to sleep. I am all over my body feeling like that. And I can feel something through the arms there, just like running through the hands and out the end of the fingers. After that my hands start to shaking. This happened right in the middle of the afternoon. My hands trembled all afternoon till toward sundown, then I stopped for a little while and start again after dark. I don't know how much I am doing, on account of the body, the way it feel. I was sitting over on the northwest side of the hogan and that shaking start off again. It was dark night, but I thought the sun was shining on me. I feel like the sunshine was coming in the door. The sun was shining bright like today in a little spot where I am sitting. That happened just a little while and then the sunshine moved off in the south side very quickly. Then that feeling I got in my body, I can feel it very well. It all start from the end of the toe and coming up through the knees and on up to the top of the head." (This order of progression is a pattern seen in many ceremonials and is the way things are applied to the body to drive out evil.) "I felt it in my arms, right through the arms and through the end of the fingers.

After that is all gone I felt very good. It felt good after that, all that Hand-trembling stopped then. The next day when I was out herding sheep it starts again for a little while, and then it is all over again. I had it like that one day and after that it didn't do it any more. The people around here who were with me, they all know. They told me I had the Hand-trembling like the other people knows how." However, nobody at this time asked him to do any diagnosing.

It was approximately in this fifteenth year that another event occurred which made a great difference in Jaime's life. The maternal aunt who had been taking care of him died, and her husband, Juanito, married another woman who lived about fifteen miles away, not very far from a little Mexican village. In accordance with Navaho custom Juanito moved to the home ground of his new wife, but he also did something that was not so customary when he took the nephews of his deceased wife, Jaime and Mario, along with him. For the succeeding five years, Jaime had little contact with his own race and his horizon was largely bounded by Mexicans, sheep, and Juanito. They worked on hire to the Mexican sheep owners. "I didn't know my people (Navaho) very well. The reason is I was with Mexican and herding sheep and not with my own people." Another Indian who knew him in those days said, "He was with the Mexicans all the time and saw very little of the Navahos. They used to call him 'Mexican's son.' All he knew then was sheep and Mexicans and nothing else besides." He even prayed like a Mexican.

He was taught work and obedience by Juanito. He learned how to camp and manage pack animals. "Juanito told me I should be cook. Right at the beginning I burn all my bread up, burn the meat, too. But Juanito tell me how to do it every time I make a mistake. I stay with the job till I learn how to do it, and after that I am a good cook." He learned how to herd sheep so they would fatten, how to keep them in good condition and take care of them at lambing time so as to get a large crop of living lambs. He learned about shearing and breeding and how to drive the sold sheep slowly across seventy-five miles of semi-arid country so they would arrive at the railroad in fine shape.

He had good relationships with his Mexican employers. "The man that own the sheep came to see us once in a while. He says I was a good cook. He wanted to see if we needed anything, that is, groceries or sheep salt, and if I did needed some at the camp he would send it right up. He used to say, 'I want to put a lot of food at the camp, I don't like to let the herders go hungry, I want them to eat lots and have good clothes to wear so my sheep will be taken care of very good for me.' He used to tell Juanito that we must take care of the sheep like we owned them." Juanito received $30.00 per month and his food and Jaime got $20.00 and food.

There was little play or amusement in the life. Juanito laid stress on earning a living. When in a mood to reminisce, he would tell Jaime and Mario about his childhood which was one of hunger and want. They had dug a small plot of ground with the shoulder blade of a cow, and by sheer hand labor raised enough crops to live on. Corn and little else had been their food, until they had moved near a village and got work herding for the Mexicans. Then food and clothes had become adequate and Juanito in time had built up a flock of his own.

Out with the sheep or minding the camp, Jaime had little to think about except the importance of subsistence. He would watch the shadows on the earth so he would know when to have the meals ready for Juanito. Jaime evidently feels much in debt to Juanito. "Me and my brother, Juanito raise us, he told us a lot of mind when we was a little child. My father didn't tell us anything. But Juanito, when he says anything to us, he talk like we are his children. He used to say 'My son' to me. He can say 'My son' to me yet."

Nevertheless, Jaime made it clear that he felt he had been exploited by Juanito to some extent. After Jaime had herded for him for many years, Juanito only gave him fifteen sheep. When they had worked for the Mexicans, Juanito took Jaime's wages, although he bought him clothes. Once Juanito tried to make Jaime and his brother Mario work off a debt that Juanito owed a Mexican, but the Mexican would not let the boys do it.

One day when Jaime was about twenty, a messenger came to Juanito seeking to arrange a marriage between Jaime and a girl in one of the most influential Navaho families of the region. Juanito debated the matter and then agreed without much consideration of Jaime's wishes. The very next day found a somewhat bewildered and abashed Jaime being conducted to his wedding by some of his relatives who drove the sheep and led the horse with the silver bridle that were gifts for the girl's family. The wedding was a very formal affair, with a full-fledged ceremonial in a large hogan and a great many people present. Jaime said that if he had known what it was going to be like, he would not have come. There was a feast spread with all kinds of meat and bread, and the bride's father made a speech. He told the girl she was married now to Jaime, had a home of her own and must take care of it. She must wash the dishes, sweep the floor, and take care of the fire, and mind what Jaime told her to do. Then he gave Jaime similar advice and said the two of them should do their best to make a good home. He said, "Some places where they have a wedding, they don't get along very good, but I want you to get along. Do the farming, make a good house, do the outside work, do the work for your own. Sometimes you can work for Mexican or white people, and mind all those people who you work for. Try and get along the best way you can with all your people. Through the summer what you raise, harvest your crop, store them away for the winter time and try to save all your money if you can. Won't be long before you going to have some children."

After the ceremony, in accordance with Navaho custom, Jaime remained with his wife and her people and began to herd their sheep. Soon he discovered that the girl did not pay much attention to the speech that her father had made. "Every time I come in I have to do my own cooking. The girl talks back and says she don't want to do it." She would not even come camping with him when it was necessary to take the sheep to fresh pasture. After some time he went to her family. "I told the people that if they want me to keep on herding, I want a little money every month for my trouble. If the girl will come to the camp and help me like her father told her to, then I would do the herding for nothing."

The girl's family said that they would hold a meeting in four days' time to discuss it. Jaime said that he would be there, but he would not do any talking then. At the meeting the girl's father gave her a public lecture, and then some other men spoke to her. In the end she said that she would go to the sheep camp with him. When she got down there Jaime discovered that she did not know how to cook, so he taught her, and after that they got along moderately well for a while.

From that time on Jaime was in closer contact with his own people after his five years of partial separation. In telling his life story he makes a great point of how much he knew about sheep and how he improved the methods the other Indians were using and how they admired him and tried to secure his services a year in advance for the lambing season. He also continued his work for the Mexicans occasionally.

In the course of time, trouble with his wife became worse. They had no proper home because she would not stay in their hogan. She said she liked to go around where people were living and she did not see why she should stay home when Jaime could be out all the time. He told her that he was getting pay for being out herding, and asked who paid her for running around, but she would not listen. "Any time I talk like that to her, she goes out." So he let her alone and spent the winter out with the sheep. "While I am herding, I forgot about this woman. I thought the best way for me to do is to stay with the sheep like always and let the woman suit herself. In the spring I brought the sheep back home. The woman was more mad yet, she had a young baby."

About this time, in his twenty-third year, his marital trouble was well known and doubtless relished and gossiped about. He was beginning to live like a Navaho again instead of a Mexican, but he was ignorant of Navaho ways and knew few people. And yet he was interested in the opinion that his fellows had of him as indicated by the way he talked of the impression he made on them as a herdsman. It was under these circumstances that he began to practice diagnosis by Hand-trembling.

You will recall that he had the Hand-trembling sickness some years before and others had told him that now he should be able to diagnose, but no one had hitherto asked him to perform. One day a messenger came asking him to come at once to see his uncle Manuel, who had been ill for some time, with his legs swollen, which made him unable to walk. A number of people had done Hand-trembling and a number of Singers had held ceremonials, but Manuel was no better. When he arrived, Jaime said that Manuel asked him to do the Hand-trembling. "He told me he wanted me to try it out. He says he will give me a good sheep. I told him I don't know much about Hand-trembling. That is something I just had. He told me I better try it. Well, I made up my mind and did it for this man for quite a while. I found out he have to get a Singer who know the Apache Wind Way ceremonial. I told them they should get Ricardo."

When we asked Jaime how he found this out, he said, "When you going to do the Hand-trembling, first you close your eyes, you hold your hand out and start to thinking. You say a few words in pray. When you close your eyes you feel something like lightning or sunbeams coming from heaven, strike down inside the house, everything is white and bright. Nobody could see that but you. You don't (actually) see that yourself, but you having thoughts like that. That light doesn't stay long, then your hand starts shaking. You start thinking about Singers' names, taking them one at a time. As you go along the Hand-trembling kind of pushes the Singers off. Then you come to one and the Hand-trembling will push him right inside the house. That is the way I did it, and when I come to Ricardo it push him in.

"About this white sunbeam, if you didn't have that, it is bad luck. When you get the white shining bright, that is good. When you feel the patient and everything is black in the house, that means no good, you are going to lose the patient.

"This isn't like a man come (to a doctor) and he asks questions, this is thinking hard. We must go by this trembling hand. Whenever you start your hand trembling, do not try to hold it back, let it go and see what it will do. Just foller your arm, like."

When asked how he selected the right ceremonial after having picked the Singer, Jaime said, "The Singers have got sand paintings. The Hand-trembling drawed out the sand painting of the sun. In that ceremonial they use the cactus. I draw that cactus, too. This is the way I find out."

It is worth noting that there are a limited number of Singers in the region, that each of these knows only a few ceremonials, that Jaime's knowledge of religious lore was not extensive, and that many Singers and ceremonials had already been tried. This means that the number of new suggestions that Jaime could make were limited.

Manuel got Ricardo and Ricardo sang as directed by Jaime. "Manuel was real sick when Ricardo started, was swell all over on both legs. After Ricardo sang a day and a night, the man begin to get well. From the finish of the ceremonial, just five days after that, the man beginning to walk around. He got better every day until he got well."

Jaime's wife didn't think much of his powers. "She says I have no sense doing that, shaking hands for somebody. She thinks I am crazy to do that. But I don't pay any attention to the woman, I go on with my work."

One day a man came with a story that his wife had been having trouble giving birth to a baby. Singers and Hand-trembling experts had come from all over, even from the other side of the Zuni mountains, and nobody could do the woman any good. "They sure need a good man for the Hand-trembling over that woman. He says he want to pay me a good saddle horse for do that." Jaime went to see the woman and found she had been in labor for five days. There was a large crowd of people at the place. He hung a red woman's belt over the patient and sprinkled her with corn pollen.

"I say I don't want all that crowd in there, they can all go out for a while. I need three women in there, that is all. After I start Hand-trembling, I got up and put my hand on the woman's belly where the baby lay and push it down. First I start very easy and then I go harder with it. The woman had a big pain. I still had the Hand-trembling, helping her with it. I quit and called the men in. I told them the baby was all right, laying head downwards, and coming at the right time. I told them the baby will come in about an hour, maybe not so long. The people didn't believe it, they had tried five days already and four other men had done Hand-trembling. They think the baby is not still living yet. I said that I had tried my best with Hand-trembling and that was the way I got it. The woman have big pain again, I start the Hand-trembling again and do like I did before, pushing down. The woman had the baby right away, and the placenta came at the same time. The baby looked good, cried good, was in good shape. Everybody is surprised."

They fed Jaime royally and gave him the horse. It was a good black one. "When I bring this horse home, my wife says it is going to be hers. She didn't get mad about it that time."

From then until the present he has continued to practice Hand-trembling in the community. From remarks we heard by others, there can be no doubt that he is considered one of the most successful. In the course of his life story he gave us many descriptions of his performances all of which had in common the facts that the patient was very ill; that nobody knew what to do till Jaime told them; that he had great Singers doing his bidding; that the patient got well; that everybody was surprised and pleased; and that Jaime was well paid.

The marriage lasted after a fashion for four years. Then Jaime says, "The woman quit me. Didn't say for what. She wants to quit, that's all. She told me to go home to Juanito's place. So I went back home and I never did go back down there to her place after that."

As the years went by he added farming to his skill as a sheep man, and then, working for a white rancher, learned to handle cattle. "I like that man. When I start to work for him on cattle, I was afraid the cows might hook me, but after I got used to it, I like to be a cowman."

In the fall of 1932, when Jaime was about thirty, there was a great crop of wild pinyon nuts in the region where he lived. Indians came from all the country round to pick the nuts, and many families spent the winter there camping. Among these was a woman from Kainti and her daughter, Susan, and Jaime became friendly with them. The old lady urged Jaime and her daughter to live together, which they did. When the spring came, he went with his new wife and her mother back to Kainti and worked on the old lady's farm through the summer. He soon found out that his mother-in-law had a very bad reputation in the neighborhood. She had roped him in because she wanted his horse to help pull their wagon home, and then she tolerated him through the summer because of the work he was doing on the farm. As soon as the harvest was over she turned on him and drove him out. He made no resistance to this, but the girl had had enough of life with her mother, had found Jaime to be a man to her taste, and she told him she was going along. The two rode off without saying a word to the old woman, and they never saw her again from that day to this.

"From that time on I didn't go to work for white man or Mexican any more. I stop and settle down right there. In the winter time I live where I am living now. In summer I live about a mile and a half from here where my farm is. Every summer I raise a little crop, I make my living with that. I did some Hand-trembling different places."

This outline of the story of his life gives some hint of his temperament and personality make-up, but some aspects may be further stressed and some additional incidents pointed out. It is clear that he is shy, timid, passive, and sensitive to the opinions of others. These appear in his docility and obedience to Juanito—"What Juanito says, I mind"—; bashfulness at his wedding; refusal to speak at the meeting held over his wife's conduct; his running away from her. At religious ceremonials he was unusual in that he would not perform the ceremonial vomiting for many years. "I was bashful while all those other people was there." Not only did he run away rather than take his own part against his first wife and the mother of his second, but he allowed himself to be chased off some land he was farming by two white ranchers who got not only the land but the sheep and equipment, too. To this may be added his generally shy manner we observed and the fact that he had a ne'er-do-well maternal cousin on his hands while we were there.

It should be realized that these personality qualities are not so rare among the Navahos and are somewhat after the pattern of the culture, but it seems clear that even for a Navaho, Jaime was unusually shy, passive and timid. His great interest in the opinions of others comes out again and again when he tells how people marvelled at his skill as a sheep man and later at his powers in Hand-trembling.

STORY 11

This story was given by a Navaho woman of about fifty-five. We explained that we would like her to tell us everything she could remember from the first thing right up to the present. She left a gap from the time she was married until eight years ago. Scarcely any questions were asked during the recounting, and the story is in her words, as translated by another Navaho.

"The place was called 'White Pointed Rock.' There's a canyon out south from that place. Right in this canyon, there's where we was living. From there I started to remember. I don't know how big girl I was, but I remember pretty well.

"My mother used to grind corn on a rock, like these girls doing, between two rocks. One day she ground corn. I was around my mother playing. She finished grinding. When she was putting away the rock, she lifted it up and was going to put it against the wall. She dropped that rock on me, right on this right hip. I was pretty badly hurt. They had an Indian doctor for me and sing over me. Think that man sing about three days and three nights. Didn't get well very quick. This man only sing that much time. Then I was sick long time after that. When I got well, any time I do little heavy work, that hurt come back all the time. When I got well I can't walk very far on account of that. Most of the time my mother carried me on her back.

"Don't remember how long we lived there. We start to move from there over to another place that was called 'House on Top of the Rock.' We lived at this place two years. I got well pretty good while we living there. Then we moved too much—moved from there on back to this place we just left.

"Over there somebody had a place fenced up, and my people said to this man they wanted to plant some corn in that field. Man said it would be all right with him, but not to farm all of it; he would rent them just a little patch. We planted corn there. On this little patch we raised some watermelons, corn, squash. In the summer time we lived there so we can plant our corn. In the winter time we moved in the canyon where I got hurt. They was a lot more people living right around this place.

"The places where we wintered and summered, we move back and forth between these for many years. We own little bunch of sheep and goats. Sing like what they had last night, Blessing Way Sing, people having Sings in that Way mostly at that time.

"One summer we made a trip from there on to Kainti. My oldest sister was living down there. We stayed there about one summer. When we got there my sister was sick. My oldest brother was a Singer, too, at that time. We took him down there with us. My oldest brother sung for this woman, and they were a lot of other Singers meet together and try to cure this woman, but they didn't. All that summer she has been sick; toward the fall she died. I can remember it was in the night time she died. She died inside the hogan and all the family move outside. When we move outside from the hogan, I could see it was full moon that night. That's what I remembered, too. It was full moon, so it gave us lot of light when we were out.

"After four days we moved to another place. We lived there for a few days more and then we come on back down to the place called 'House on top of the Rock.' This place was where our sheep and goats was kept while we was down there.

"My father was working over at the reservoir. A lot of men were working on the reservoir, and he was in the bunch. His name was José, and his wife was down there with him, that's Carmen. This lady is my sister. We got one mother and different father. After we came back here, my father came over to us. And father went back and bring his wife over, and we was living there all together. They built another hogan, there on the north side of where we was living. We move inside this hogan.

"Zunis had dance going on, that was big dance, what they call Shalako. Some people went to that dance. When we been to this dance, after that one day, a man and woman came up to our place. Man was pretty sick; the woman wasn't sick—that was his wife.

Photograph by Helen M. Post

Irrigated Land along the San Juan

Sheep at a Government Watering Trough

Photograph by Helen M. Post

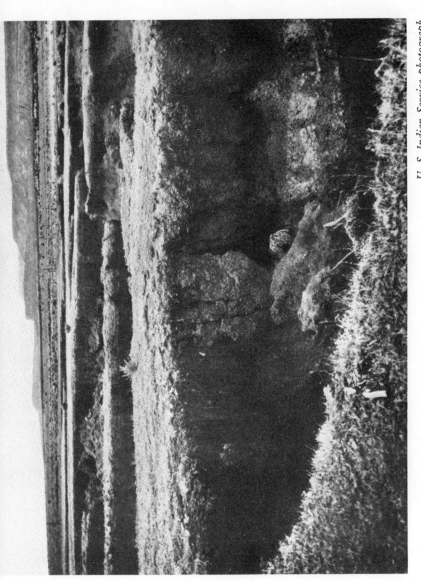

Unchecked Erosion Has Eaten Away This Formerly Level Grazing Area

When they came the woman took the horses back that they came on. She went home and he stayed there. This man is my brother, too. Next day when they was looking at him, the people says this man has something all over on his body. What he has over his body is all red. We stayed one night with this man, all of us. Next morning my father took us to another place. Father says that was pretty bad to stay near that man, says we might get it from him. What he has on his body is getting heavier every day; they found out it was small-pox.

"My father got afraid to go over to this man, but my mother wasn't afraid. She went over and took care of this sick man. She stayed with him two days. After two days we heard she got it, too. The sick man and my mother and my father, they was the only ones talked together. When my mother come to us she could just walk behind the doorway here and talk to us. My father told them not to come in. Some of our folks have fixed some food up for them, and they can just put it outside and carry it out to them. The man that came up first, he's getting better, but my mother is getting worse again. She got too worse, and she has it all over her body, sores all over, and died; didn't live long.

"One of my oldest brothers was a Singer, too. He came in there just about the time my mother died. He got it right away again. He didn't get it very bad; he got better on that. They used some kind of medicine and was been drinking, rubbing on their bodies in the sweat house. They got well. The two men got well and my mother died.

"Everybody got afraid to go near the hogan, so they didn't bury her but just left her inside the brush hogan. Father says when they ready to leave her they cut a lot of pinyon limbs and cover her up good with it and close the hogan. They move away from there right away.

"The two men, that they got well, they don't come in on us; they keep their camp on one side. They do that for quite a while until they think they was sure well. After they thought they was sure well, they did come back to their people.

"We move from there to another place. This place was called 'Snake Water.' We stayed about a year there. From there we moved to old man Sam's place.

"This old man Sam is my brother. The two women were sisters; one of them was the mother of Sam, the other was my mother. So I called him brother. Old man Sam told us to move down there so we could plant some corn on his place. We lived there, I don't quite remember just how long it was, a few years anyway. We moved just this side of Sam's place.

"My father start to herding sheep for a man, man's name Herrera. This was white man. This man owned a lot of sheep. My father herd sheep around there for a short time, then this white man move his sheep to Albuquerque. So my father, he stayed with the sheep—he moved to Albuquerque, too. He stayed one year down there. We had it pretty hard up that year. Nobody was taking care of us; we was all by ourselves. We go pretty hungry that year, go without shoes, didn't have much clothes to wear, hardly any blankets to sleep with. We make our living through the winter the best way we can; but we was all alive when my father came back, none of us starved.

"I remember that summer a lot of pinyon all over in here. There was a lot of yucca fruit the same time. In the fall we picking pinyons and putting up some yucca fruit. What pinyons we pick, we don't have to take to the store; we used to keep them for the winter time. There is wild seed, what we call 'grass seed.' A lot of these wild seeds, we eat them, too. There's a lot of wild cherries, too. We been picking these.

"I was about as big as one of these two girls (thirteen years old). I can herd sheep all by myself. I must have been pretty good herder, didn't lose any sheep. Some other days, I take care of home while the other people goes out and looks out for some wild seeds.

"We was living with old man Sam. We had a hard time in one year till my father came back home. When my father came back from Albuquerque, he says he didn't herd all that time; herd part of the time and the rest of the time stay to do work at the ranch, the ranch that belongs to this man that owns the sheep. The time that he stay around the home he do the washing for the white people, and haul wood, chop wood.

"We lived there for three years. My father was raising some corn. After three years we move away from there, on the west side from there, to a place not far away, called 'Wild Rose.' I think it was the only place where they had those wild roses. We stayed another year there; then moved out south not very far from there. That place was called 'Little White Hills.' We been living there for some time. I herd all the time. When we been living there just little over one year, we move back to old man Sam's place.

"We live there mostly in summer time, so our father could take care of the crop. But we moved around in the winter time; right around old man Sam's place, we been moving all the time in the winter time, never very far away. Another place we used to move, just this side of town. Old Lady Carmen, we was moving together; we was living all together at that time, the children what she has, all raised up over there.

"There was a white man living there at that time. This white man used to be married to Mexican woman. My father used to work for that man quite a lot. We get along with these people pretty well. We used to weave for this man and woman. He gets different colored yarn, brings it to us. We weave pretty near that size rug (3 by 5 feet), the rest of them little ones. Don't remember what they used to pay for it. Juanito was moving around with us, Juanito and another man. They went out and start herding for a Mexican man; they been herding about two years for a Mexican. When they came home they brought a bunch of sheep. They was used to say when they was going to get paid, they don't want to take the money, rather take the sheep, so this man paid them off in sheep.

"These two men stayed home for a little while. They went back the same place, start herding for that same man again. The sheep what's brought in, they put it together with our sheep. Father start herding that sheep, and we also help herd. Every year when these sheep lambing, we all help together after they quit lambing. Father herds the sheep all the summer time. In the fall time the wether lamb we trade back to Mexican with the ewe lamb. We get the ewes. In that way we made a big herd every year.

"There's Carmen, Juan's first wife, Juanito, and myself, and old man Sam. These people were working together at that time. Juanito wasn't married. I used to have an older sister. We was begin to be herder long that time. I don't remember how long we herd, but about six years.

"There were no earmarks on the sheep at all. Nobody asked us how many sheep we owned in the bunch. Juanito was boss of the sheep all the time. After that Juanito put the earmark on all the sheep. After that we told him we want to earmark our sheep like he did. Old man said didn't want to have the sheep earmarked different ways. 'Let's run it this way,' he says, 'all have one earmark, and all of you people help take care of the sheep; you own some sheep just the same.'

"When me and my sister was herding out, we seen a woman on a horse pretty near every day. Always come to us, talk to us. She was been doing that, I think, so she come together with Juanito. We heard that this woman and Juanito, they was going to married. They just come up together, talk there together, didn't have any ceremonial about it. After that we still herding; Juanito also herd again. That woman, she just stay around home, take care of the home while we herding.

"This woman has a few goats out somewhere. She was living down below over here, where Leon living now, down around there. The goats that she brought into this flock, she owns.

"We move over here then at that time, right out about two miles south away from here. The sister that was herding with me got married just about that time. That woman, Juanito's wife, she helps me herd again in place of my sister.

"Man named Julio married my sister. The time when I started to remember very well, myself and my sister, we was always together. Anything we do, we always work together. After Julio married my sister, then we was split up. After that Juanito's wife is right there with me again. After that Julio's mother moved their home where we are living. We were living all together right that one place. Then Juanito come back; he herding again.

"I don't know how many years Julio and his mother was living there with us; I think it was about four years they been living together, Julio and his mother and his wife, they move back over here, Big Fields.

"I was the only one give more help to Juanito than anybody else, so I thought I had more sheep in the herd than anybody else. When Julio and his wife left, five more years after that, Juanito's wife says we separate our goats. We says, 'All right,' so they separate twenty goats first, which we was own before we put the sheep together. Juanito and his wife says that's all we own. We try hard to get part of the sheep, but we couldn't do it. The reason we couldn't, they got no earmarks. We just took the twenty head of goats with us and left Juanito.

"We live separate from Juanito after that. Carmen had a bunch of goats at that time, so we put that twenty head back with Carmen's goats. One or two more years, I come back to Juanito and begin to herd again. I help there; didn't stay very long, and another woman came there. This woman has a bunch of sheep, too. She told me she want me to herd for her. That made me leave Juanito. She took me back to her home and I start to herd for that woman from there on.

"I was about this girl's size (thirteen years) when I went to that woman. When I was here about one year, little over one year, that woman is kind of mean, after I got used to her. She wants me to do hard work all the time. She used to have a husband, but that time this woman she told me that I could married her husband. She tried to quit that man.

"My family was living over here just this side of Cielo. When this woman start to talk about me that way, I was herding with a girl about this size (ten years). In the evening when we was bringing the sheep to the hogan, I told the girl that I was going home, she can take the sheep. The woman came next morning. She wanted me to go back and herd for her some more, but I was afraid to go back with her. All my family wanted me to go back with that woman but I didn't want to. They wanted to know why I come back home, but I didn't say anything about what the old woman says. The woman went back home by herself. Her husband came over two days after that, wanted me to herd down there again, but I didn't go back. I wanted to stay home. I remember one or two times the old lady come back over for me, but I didn't go.

"When I was down there with the old lady she told me to card out the wool, spin out, work on the wool all the time. First when I begin this I didn't know how to work the wool, but she teach me all about it—how to card it out first, then spin it, then get it up between the loom, and start weaving a little. I didn't know how to weave, how to put design in it; know just a very little. I got that far with it and start to run away. If old lady didn't start to talking that way, I would have stayed longer.

"I was living with Carmen. She asked me whether I know how to weave. Told her I knowed a little, not much. Her and her sister put up a blanket for weave. Start to teach me again how to weave, how to put design in it. That is how I learned how to start to weave then.

"From this side of Cielo where we were living, from there we moved out south about six miles away, over where Carmen is living now.

"We moved from there one place to another, just a little way apart. In the summer time we lived over there where Carmen lives now. That's our farm place. In the winter time, from fall, we are over where the Mexican lives, below the Mexican and across; there were some Mexicans have some sheep out south from here, about nine or ten miles away. When they start lambing, father used to take us there and herd the sheep while they lambing. We herd till one and a half months. That's only lambing time. And when we get our pay we come back here again. This is only two different times we herd out there.

"Last time when we herd out there for the Mexican, this one of the sisters that married Julio, this same woman, was down there with us herding sheep. But she got bitten by snake while we're herding there. Bit her right on this toe (big toe). We was herding together one day, walking through the malapai rocks. I seen the snake first, it was a rattle snake, laying down before us. I run off this way and pointed over there. I thought she seen the snake, but she run right where the snake was, lying down. Snake was too close for her; she run over it and step on it, and that's how the snake got a hold of her toe. She dragged that snake for a little while, tried to kick it off, but the snake wouldn't drop. After a while it turned her loose. She was wearing a moccasin of buckskin, and when she pulled the shoe off, it was full of blood inside the moccasin. She just sat down right there. She send me to tell father. We know our father is at the camp; he help cook for all the herders.

"I ran to the camp and seen my father there; told him about it right away. The Navaho had their camp one side, the Mexican on the other; camp two different places. We told Mexican about this. Father ran over there where my sister was. He told me to wait till the Mexican start to go over there with the wagon. When the Mexican start with his buggy down there, I went with the Mexican to show him where the place was. When I went along with the Mexican, my father had got there before we did. Before I went off to the camp we see the snake over in a hole under the rock. The Mexican ask where the snake went; I showed them where it went. Mexican dug the hole up and the snake wasn't very far in the hole. They found the snake and killed it. The woman got into the wagon then and we went back to the camp.

"When we came back to the camp, before we left over there where they killed the snake, they tied her leg up tight with a string about the knee. Mexican say he think he know a medicine that will cure that right away. Father told Mexican, he think he know a man can cure that, too, a Navaho man. This man, we was living with him, that knows the medicine. My father asked the Mexican if he could take the woman home in his buggy right away. Mexican says, "Yes," and start to take her home in the buggy. When we got home we told this man that knows the medicine about it. He got that medicine, and I think the medicine is good. It was swelling pretty bad; after she took the medicine the swelling began to go down. But she didn't use her foot for two weeks after that. After two weeks she began to walk on that foot all right. I seen the medicine. There's two kinds;

one was yucca root, the other a plant about that size (1½ inches in diameter), and the leaves of it was pretty sharp. I seen the medicine; it was dark color all over. Medicine man says, wherever these grow, if it touches your hand it will make it swell up for a little while. Sometime ago when I was out with this girl (married daughter) in the canyon out back of Carmen's, I saw a plant just like the medicine. I put my hand on the medicine; it was pretty sharp, and right away a swelling on my hand. I kneeled down on the medicine with my knees; did just the same again. When we came back that night, this leg was still swelled; put on a pretty good sized swell, and stayed same place till we got home.

"We didn't know the name. These peoples that knows this medicine, they don't want to tell anybody the name of it. In the summer I wouldn't tell about it, either. This is winter time, so I am telling about it. The medicine man won't tell anybody about this medicine, except only if some one had the snake bite real bad, then he'll tell just that one. They don't like to talk about it.

"From then we been moving from one place back to another, right from here in a small space. From that time till we start living here. We been moving on this place about eight years ago. We didn't plant very good field all the places where we been move. But after we move on this place we begin to raise pretty good crop pretty near every year. All through that time where we been plant corn, we plant somebody else's place. We got our own place now. We like this place pretty well. That's about all.

"After we move on this place, I got sick one time pretty bad. I don't remember how much medicine people did for me. I don't know what sickness I had, but I acted like a drunk person. I don't know a thing what I was doing hardly. This was going on about two years. The last of it they sung Hand-Trembling Way for me; man's name Fred, I think. That cured me after all. Sing three different times for me. First time did it five nights and four days, second time three nights and one day, third time five nights and four days. That's three different times. Told me I need one more time to get all over it. We are too poor, so we don't put another one. Like to finish through with it, but we can't. My mind acts just like a drunk person's, and besides I get a pain up in one of my shoulders, and my arm I can't hardly move. My mind was bad. My mind all right now, only my back gets a little pain."

This woman knew her own mind from the time she was a young girl, perhaps because of her mother's death and being thrown on her own resources—living with relatives, to be sure, but earning her own keep for the most part. She gives a picture of Juanito which fits rather well with that in Story I, in which he tried to have Jaime and Mario work off his debt to the Mexican. She evidently resented the treatment she received much more than did Jaime, who, of course, could balance the exploitation against all the time Juanito had spent training him to be a good shepherd. Both Jaime and this woman, however, were well aware that something was put over on them. This sort of situation was common in our own society until child labor laws stopped it and our general economic level rose to where exploitation of dependents was less necessary. She did not fight bitterly against Juanito, she simply removed her stock from his.

One wonders why she was silent about her married life, which filled many years. Was it forbidden to speak of it? Was it too painful or too intimate an experience? One can only guess. She disposes of it in a single paragraph, with no mention of husband and children and their common joys and sorrows. When asked if she would tell more about it, she replied that "she guessed she would let it go," and went on to describe an illness she had had.

Jaime did the same thing for his present marriage, although he described the one that failed with many details. It is probably a matter of reticence in dealing with affection and the expression of it.

STORY III

This man is a Curer of about fifty, who traded his story for some stories we told him about war and the wonders of the world.

"I was told by my mother that I was born right two and a half miles east from Smith's place, that little canyon. I used to know the place, the hogan. One time I see the hogan, and another time I seen nothing on the place, all rot away. The last what I saw there was the place where the hogan used to set, the dirt was piled around it. Doesn't show any more at this time. I was born in summer, right next to the middle, along in July; just about the time the top of the corn begin to tossel out.

"Now this is about my life story, which I remember. At this time this would be my beginning, right in the same canyon, little way up from that hogan. I remember the place where we was living, me and my oldest sister was together at home. The head of the family and all the rest wanted to go some place. They said we should look after the hogan and take care of things. We was doing this in the day time. Right up till after dark, and it begins sundown, we was afraid. There was another hogan nearer than that. We were quite afraid at night an owl or a spirit would get us, so we went to the other hogan and slept there to someone else's home. We did this for a few days.

"I remember we never moved long way from there, only living there for many years. Same time we were planting corn every summer; we planted squash also. We always used to raise pretty good crop, and back in that time it rained quite often, so people raise pretty good corn and squashes, watermelon, muskmelon, what we don't plant now. Through that rainy time the country was very good. The grass was growed so high and the sunflower was so high they was little over a pony.

"Same time I was herding with another herder. I was just with him, of course; I don't herd very good. Wasn't very good herding, this high grass and sunflower. For that reason we used to move so the sheep can go better. Grass is about like that in summer. Then when the winter times come, I suppose what grass and sunflower was left to ripe, the seeds of that used to fall and make a crop for another year. That the reason the grass was so high.

"We used to go up in the hill for a short time; we can camp there; take one day to kill a deer and bring out the deer for meat, and same with antelope. Those days we don't have to go far for deer and antelope. They was raised right along in the country.

"From that time I was herding with my older sister. When we was herding daytime, had some dogs with us. Was so many rabbits that the dogs could run up the rabbits into a hollow, into a hole, and we can get the rabbits out of the wood (log), and this the way we was killing the rabbits. The rabbit was very fat then. Those days these logs, lot of logs, had hollows in them. At this time (1940) it is pretty hard to get that kind of log with the hollow in it. The people have chopped it up for firewood every place.

"From then I begin to herd by myself; I know more about herding. Next thing I do was to herd with a pony; can ride a horse then pretty good and that's what I herd with. They send me out to look for horses. They let the horses go at night and next morning they send me out to see if I can bring them in. Sometimes I found the horses and sometimes I didn't—come back without them.

"When I come up to there, people was farming. I couldn't farm by myself, but I could help the other people to plant. They didn't have no plows nor hoes which they can digging with. They had stick about two feet long. This was the stick was called for digging. They point one end, flat and sharp. And I watched the people, how they plant the corn and squash with this. Some of these days while I go home, while nobody else is home, I stole some of those squash seeds which was belonged to the head of the family. The oldest man in the bunch knows how to plant the way I got it in my mind. I used to put a little manure with corn or squash and put it in the soft wet dirt and cover it. This was the way they was used to plant. I carried these seeds out there to the field and planted there by myself. That's what I learned over there. Today that's what I am doing yet, planting with horse manure, not the corn, just the squash seed. I think the horse manure will carry the moisture long, never goes dry.

"Then from that time my people move out this way, all through here where you can see these hills toward Tall Mountain. We hadn't got anything to move with, only horseback. Don't quite remember how much load they pack on horse. Now these days I can see a lot of load in one home. I know the load what we was carry on horse that time was quite high on top the horse. Small children, they used to ride on top the load; they used to ride double or three. Whenever the horse steps in a ditch or hole, the first thing we do with him is fall off the horse, and whenever that happens the pails or any dishes on the horse they start rattling and scare the horse and it start running, bucking, kicking, and all we do is to cry there where we fall. We start to moving again when they catch that horse back and put the load on top and put the children on top.

"Those days we used to have a lot of pinyon crop, also a lot of rat nest of pinyon. We could use the rat nest which was always piled up by the rats. Used to have many rat nests in the country at that time; now there is hardly any more. What I used to kill was rabbit, and also porcupine, as I cannot kill the big game at all yet, that is, the deer and antelope.

"The head of the family told us to herd the sheep more and take care of the horses, water the horses and haul some water with the horse—take up two little jug and put it on each side of the saddle and bring in some water. Around our home, when we are old enough, able enough to do, we got to do it whatever he told us. From that time I can begin to think about things what I can do.

"We mind what the head of the family says. (Who was the head?) Father and mother. If we didn't mind just like what he says to us, he could get a whip and start to whipping us till we do it. Then along in the winter time, when the snow is on the ground, in the fall time when the first snow come, when the snow is deep enough to roll in it, they told us to roll in the snow, or else to run race quite a ways from the hogan where there is water and ice. When I get down there I chop the ice so I can get through to the water and swim in there for a little while. Then I run back home, warm up myself. The next thing what they said to do was get outside again, where tree branches is covered with snow. Said for us to break a branch so the snow will fall on our bodies. This was instruction for us, the way we was going to live farther on for many years, to make ourselves strong, brave, for because maybe some day we might get into something that is really bad, or war. If I did all these things I could go right through it, not afraid of anything.

"At that time I did all these, and another thing that they told us we should do, both for the boys and girls, is to run the race for quite a distance, starting from half a mile, that's toward daylight, just before dawn. People will tell them throw their blankets away and tell them to take their clothes off. They had some kind of a cloth about six inches wide that was given them to wear between the legs, so they can pull their clothes off. First, they only run a little ways and then run a little farther and farther, and sometimes they go two miles, that far and back. We did this, too.

"At that time they used to whip their children. So I knowed they was going to whip us. The head of the family made the first talk, and if he made the second time, that's the whip, then; so we must go by whatever he says. This will be good lesson and instruction for the children to make themselves strong and brave. For all this rolling in the snow, breaking branches, swimming in the water, that is so we can go through what anybody be afraid of, but we won't be that way. For the running races, any time when any kind of war going to get you, you can run out of it. They told us, 'This is for your own instruction, as many years as you going to live. And another thing what you doing this for is, when you get old enough to marry, you can get married and from there on you can get good living out of it, and also you can teach your children.'

"I am doing all these things what he says, follow the things what he wants me to do; whenever I come back from herding, start going for horses again. I don't do one thing and come back and stay in the hogan. Nowadays, the children like I was back in that time, I can see they don't do that any more what I did, in the summer time and the winter time and it's cold weather.

"In that time, when they kill a mutton, they don't let us eat the good meat or fat, or fat what's in the bone. We can only eat the lungs, not much of the meat; we cannot drink the soup. If we eat these things they say it will make us sleep, couldn't get up early, make us tired, want to lay down. If we eat this what he says, we can run and be light, we can do things quicker. He says the soup that we drink, after we drink it, we can get it up to our knees, makes our legs heavy, won't go very fast. And sleep after the sun is up— that's bad to do that. And when the eating time comes, we must sit up one way (crouching with one knee down, but knee not touching the floor), so as if the boss says something, we can run quick and get it.

"From then up I can go by all of that. So I went through the cold nights and early mornings. I remember the frost would get under my hair; I had hair which I could see all frosty when I went out in the early morning. Then I did some of these races all through my life. About rolling in the snow, I only did it when I started, four times in all; I got afraid of it. But I kept running races a few times more after that. Now at this time, about rolling in the snow, I couldn't do it to save my life. If somebody pay me for it, maybe I could and maybe not.

"We was living back over here at these hills. First, we was living in the canyon and then we was over at this Tall Mountain and then we was living over here right above the reservoir, three or four miles east of 'Grass Onion.' Herding mostly was my job; also I work on the farm part of the time, take care of the horses. This place was the foot of the mountain.

"At that time we had the wooden fence around the field, which was very poor fence. We didn't have no wire at that time. Many times we was sent out to watch the farm, the corn, look see if anything got into it. There was some bear used to get into the corn; so that is the next thing what we was afraid of. We used to go a little ways from the hogan, get up a place where we can see the field. If there wasn't any bear around there, we can go there. The bears could get into the corn at night time, too. In those days there used to be a few hoes, not very many of them, and no bailing wire around. What we used in place of the wire, we can use a green oak tree, we can double it back. That the way we build the fence. We could use the forky pole to put it in the ground for the fence. At that time there was nobody hauling the alfalfa feed out into the country like they doing it now.

"Another thing, what I don't remember very well, at that time in that same mountain I could see, I think it was Mexican, that was driving cow team. I don't quite remember whether Mormons or Mexicans drove this kind of team. I was wondering what was they doing, kind of worried me, what in the dickens was they doing with those cow teams, whether they didn't have any horses to drive with. Seems to me the cows used to wear the copper on the point of the horns.

"At that time I been to school, once along in that time. I was about nine years old. Back in that time there wasn't hardly any snow in the winter time, just a little. Not so awful cold through the winter. Rains was what we have most of the time. Then they send me off to school at Albuquerque, which I done.

"What I told about, up to this Albuquerque school, I lay that one side and take another place, that is, to be in school. I been in school for three years study. The fourth year I got sick and been in bed for through the winter. That was 1906.

"I skip one place. In place called Canyoncito, a man's been educated there, a Navaho boy. This man came after us. He says for us to go to Albuquerque Indian School; want us to learn some lessons down there; give plenty to eat, and besides that we can eat plenty of sweet food. Good clothes to wear. So we made up our mind and go. When I got down there I feel bad about it a few days; lonesome, pretty bad. What the man told me was truth, everything what I would have. After one year and a half, that much time, we kind of forgot we were lonesome. We can get along better then.

"I thought when I first came, the punishment that I went through already was all over; but two years when I been to school I found some more lessons yet. Boys and girls, the ones that don't mind what employees says, they could get the punishment for it. We would be in the school, but part of the time we can practice something else. That was being soldiers with the gun. Line up with it different ways, learn how to handle gun, like we being soldiers. This was sure hard thing for me to do. The most hard thing was to do this in the morning early while it was cold; hands cold on the guns. We got more than one captain to take care of these soldiers. Then we boys was made a lot of mistakes when we doing that. Sometimes we don't take the right step like they wanted us to. The ones that don't know how to do, the captain would go up to this boy and take him by the shoulders and shake him and tell him to do like the way he was told to do. The ones that are making a lot of mistakes, they can be punished for it.

"And I remember the girls was lined up for marching, and I do not know what they was doing, so I suppose they was doing something else. The man put in charge of all this was Mr. Corporal.

"Like they do this soldier marching, here is the little boys in a bunch lined up along, and there is the little higher ones, and more higher, till up to the big boys. Each bunch will have one man to take care of them. When we lined up they used to call our names. When we hear our name we holler; in that way they couldn't miss one. If they couldn't find one, they lined us up at the bed room and call out names again. If they couldn't find him then, he is run off or went home. Look around some more next day. After that when they find him run away, they could send for him, they could bring him back in a few days. These boys and girls was from different countries—some from Fort Defiance, some from Gallup, some were Lagunas.

"When anybody run back home and was brought back to the school they could be punish by jail. They had a little jail, wasn't very good. A boy could be kept there three days before they put him back in school. Around the school, where you do a little mistake, they put you in the jail, too. I remember some of the boys which was run away and was brought up back to the school, and after they give them that much punish they still want to make it worse, they give them more punish after that, so they learn and won't get by with it. At that time they used to whip some school boys.

"At that time they used to teach us a lot of works—to being carpenter, how to study, work in tailor shop, making clothes, sweep up the floor in the dormitory, how to work in the dining room, and some work how to be engineer. And how to set the windows in house, and doors. All that work, I didn't pay it any attention at that time. When I came back from there a few years after that, sometimes I been think lot all through that. I think it was very good, kind of felt sorry I didn't keep on with it. What made me leave that school was sickness.

Photograph by Helen M. Post

Health Education in the Field

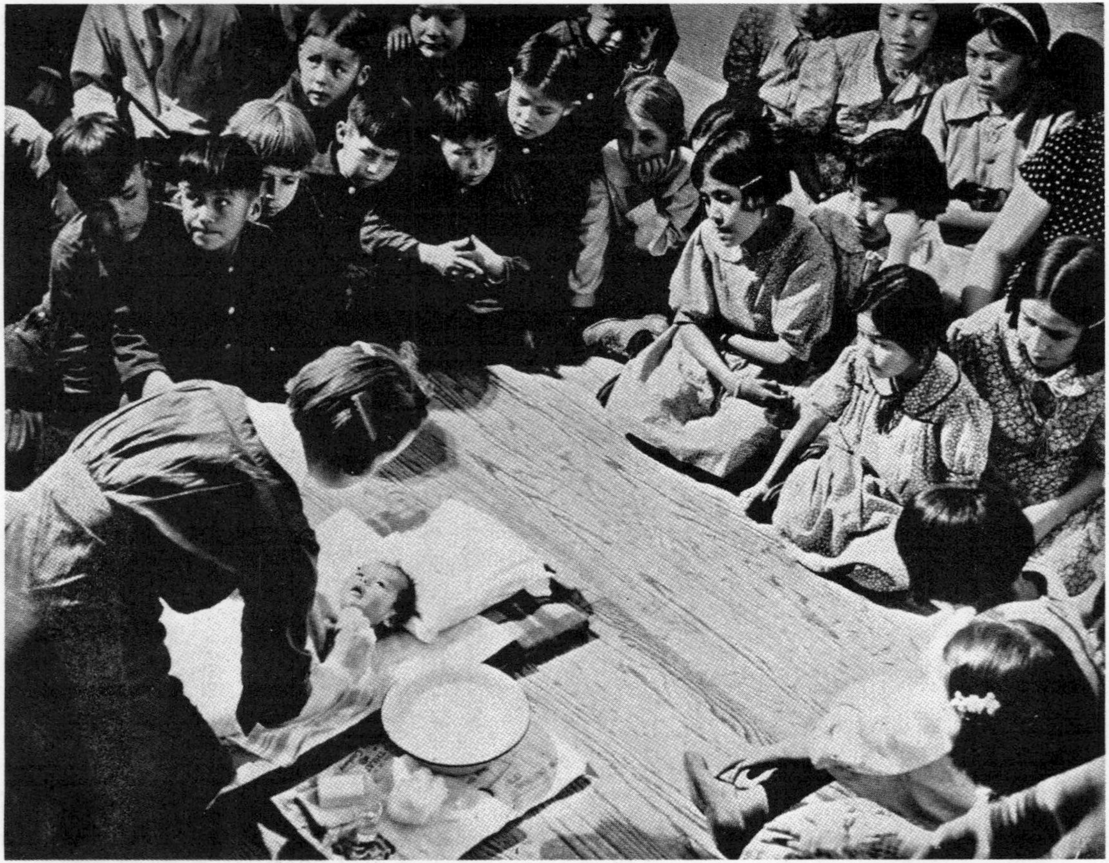

"I think that time they used to teach lots of things to the school boys and girls. Government used to have good school. The boarding school was very good for the Indian children. Nowadays they trying to put day schools. Places where they going to put day schools people don't do much about it; all they can do is to talk about it back and forth. Our children can get no place in that way. The time when I was in the school they used to watch us pretty close; they wouldn't allow us talk our own language, make us talk English, make us speak quiet in the dining room while we eating, also in bedroom. Anybody talk in school room, they tie a piece of rag around the mouth and back of his head; in that way the school children used to mind and learn their lessons. Nowadays I go through these dayschools, and where I been already watch the children, they can be yelling in their own language, hollering; in the night time they can be singing their language as loud as they can—they doing all this 'stead of learning their lessons. The teachers and employees, they can just watch the children, how much holler, how much singing, don't say not one word to the children; that's all they do is to watch and listen. That made me think that the school which we was been at that time was good school. They used to tell us not to chew tobacco or drink, and more besides, what we should not do.

"Our superintendent used to tell us we going to have some company or visitors will come and visit us. The people who came, maybe one of the men will make a speech for the children, and they should listen to it. I always listen to that myself. There was some missionaries that used to come there, too, the Catholic, he used to make talk for the children, too.

"They used to have baseball and football, both games. The people was saying the best team they got was in Albuquerque, for both games. These were the big boys and they could beat any team in the country, both football and baseball.

"When I quit school I come back to the same place. It was in early spring, May, when I came back. I was with the people again this side of town, about two miles south. The people was scattered out this way. About herding, taking care of the horses, the way they was treating me, rolling in the snow, whipping me, that was all over with me when I came back from school. By my own way I was taking care of my own horses from then on.

"By that time at my home they got some sheep, which I might herd one day when I came back. Then I can see some wagons, not very good looking. The reason they was not very good looking was, they was secondhand. I can see some plows, too, but they don't know how to use them. They could use hoe in place of plow. They didn't know how much work they could do with a plow, so they thought they· could do more with a hoe, better than they could do with a plow. I can plant by myself and hoe the field. I can do some heavy work then, like hauling wood, harvesting our corn, and any time when we want to harvest the corn or roast it in a pit, I can do that kind of job, too. After we get the corn this way (on cobs in a bin), dry it and shell it out with a stick.

"I can see that horses, when I ride double with somebody else, start to pitching with me. I think that very good thing; I want to learn that. I practiced this job again, breaking horses. I started to corral some horses and put the saddle on them and ride them. A few times they throwed me off; after that I learned how to do it. These wasn't very big horses what I start with; just a yearling or two year old. The farther on I go with it, get a bigger horse. I learned all these horses; they all got different way mean to it. Some horse will bite, another will kick, another will roll with the saddle on, can't make him get up. I don't know what kind of horse is easy to break, that doesn't kick, doesn't bite hardly, doesn't roll with the saddle much. Well, I learn all that about riding of these different kinds of horses. Some are easy riding, some are rough riding, some don't walk very good, some are pacer. Some don't run very much, another horse can run pretty fast.

"The mule is one side of the horse, the way the mule acts. That kind of actness the mule has I never did learn. I did not even try to break the mule. So I don't know what kind of actness the mule has. I heard a man was talking about the mule. He said, 'The mule is more meaner than horse. When you going to break a mule, when you saddle it up, get on it and start off with it and it start pitching, you will soon start falling. Right while you moving to the ground, falling, the mule will kick you twelve times before you hit the ground.' I did not know whether this is true or not; this is the way I understand. I never did touch a mule in my life until just a few days ago. The woman that I married, her father has a team of mules, and he loaned me that team, and I been taking care of that mule at this time. They not mean, they very gentle, didn't try to hurt me in any way. Feed them a little at the time. And one of the mules when I put the bridle over the ears he acts like he didn't want to be bothered of the ears, although it not mean. So I think which mule I have now, taking care of, is pretty good mule. Like to own that mule.

"I go back over here to where I start on the mule. I was about nineteen years old. From then I got up so I could marry. I got married up at that time. All these things besides breaking horses, I turned that loose and start to settle down and make up my home. First work that I start to do from there is to herd sheep three months for Mexican, drawing thirty dollars a month and board. When I come back from herding, when my herding was end, I come back where my wife was living.

"From that time my wife had some kind of trouble with her. Did not know till today what sickness she had; think her mind went wrong, seems like didn't know anything; people talk to her, couldn't understand anything. First it start on her inside the hogan, but then she began running off. When she start running off, people run after her, bring her back home; and she gets worse and worse all the time. Sometimes she ran away from home, far distance, and pull her clothes all off. We were still trying to take care of her, but she didn't stay. She would be very hungry at that time and thirsty, and she go just dry. And no one could know what that sickness was.

"We put the different Sings over my wife; but she doesn't seem to get any better. At same time there was one or two more started the same again; both young girls. They once got up pretty worse so they don't know anything, then they got a little better and they stay like that for three years. There were two Singers out toward Gallup;

they come over here and do the singing for these women. They did Sing four different times for each woman, and they got better then. They got well.

"So when my wife got acting like that it made me leave. We were living pretty close up until four years. They had a Squaw Dance this side out south here three miles, and this woman had the same thing again over here where they having Squaw Dance. When we started to go back from here she been all over the place, without her clothes. They caught her and bring her home. They did something else for her, I don't know what, and she got better again, and I hear she is better now.

"Then I stay all by myself for one year, then I married again. I went from here over this high mountain, toward place they call Thompson. North side of that, that's where I married again. Live with that woman seven years. There at that time have two children and a baby. Then we had a big flu that winter, and because of that flu, lost my wife and the baby. Two children were sent to school. They are good educated now and they are at Fort Wingate.

"At that time a company was giving out the jobs to Indians. I worked three months there that way. Worked two months one place, and another place the next one, making three months. This was a job of logging, loading up the logs on the car. They raised my wages from three dollars up to five dollars. I worked steady for two months and part of another month, like to making three months. There was a big machine loading the logs and the logs was stacking up alongside the railroad. A loading man was up on the car and two other mans was down below to handle the chain, both end of the log, one man on each side, so that when they hook on that chain, can lift up the log on top of the others. One day they was doing that again. Snow was on the logs so that the log can slip pretty easy. The chain didn't slip, but they hook on the ends just as they was lifting up the log, and it began to jerk and jump and cause the other logs to slip, and somehow one log was slip out. They didn't notice it, and I was hurt by the log on my forehead. It just barely touch me where it was fall on the ground. When that log start to falling I noticed it and I started to running, but it got me. There was one log lying alongside me. The log that was falling dropped on this log alongside me, so I was safe from that log that was falling; and it hit me very little. The other man didn't notice how it happened, and we found the log fall right on top of him, the other end. After that happened we can see that he is not dead yet. He can breathe very little. Right away they take this man over to the hospital. They told me to go along, but I didn't; told them I wasn't hurt very bad, but I knowed the other man was hurt real bad. I heard that the doctor, when they bring him to the hospital, sewed a few places. They think he was not going to live, just doing the best they can for him, and he died after that. They think that the blood going into his body killed him.

"Then my people scared me, saying it wasn't a very good thing to go on with that job. So when I quit that job I come back here to my real home. From then I started to raising little crop again. That was my job at home.

"At that time our Fort Defiance Navaho agent went round different districts, inside the reservation and outside; told the people they should elect three officers, chapter officers; one will be president, one will be vice president, and one secretary. They got the land divided up some way so they can have three officers in each district. After we have heard that, my people start to do that. They point out three mens, and one was me, the vicepresident. I was helping those people for three years. Then on up three years time they changed me again to be an Indian Police.

"Then while I was being police, I was look after these people here, around at Crown Point, around Fort Defiance, around Shiprock. I am helping the police from these other different districts, wherever they have Sing going on, we looking in. At these places where I am taking care of the people it is kind of dangerous by being police. Wherever the people do wrong, drinking, or killing each other, we handle that, catch them, put handcuffs on them, and bring them to the agent at Fort Defiance or Window Rock. Somehow the people get together and talk that it wasn't right to do harm like that to the Indians what was living outside the reservation. The reason, we were elected through the Navaho Indian, through the Commissioner where there was reservation already. So I put it off for outside the reservation, the way we were handling the people. Inside the reservation we could do it yet. So some of the people beside me, they let it go. Only a few were at Fort Defiance. Right there in Gallup, in that town, they used to catch any Navaho people that was drinking and take them to Fort Defiance and jail them there. Same way with any people outside the reservation.

"About that time my father, my mother, my sister and brother, they tell me it wasn't very good job to have, they want me to stay out of it. I soon took my family and my people's word; I thought it was the best thing for me to do. And another thing, they told me I didn't do anything at my home to work for my own. So I study it over and think it over and soon I make up my mind to stay out of it. I am satisfied that I am working for the Indian, went through a lot of countries that I didn't know before; and I been to Santa Fe and out north and west and I seen the country some, and when I quit the job, when I come back to my home, I come back and stay and settle down again. Now at this time, my mother is getting old, gray-headed, can't do much work of her own, so I thought I help my mother along while she living."

This man is very different from the other two pictured in their life stories. He came from a more stable family, and had a more orderly up-bringing where purposeful discipline in accordance with the old Navaho ideals played a large part. He evidently depended on his family for guidance longer than our young people, quitting jobs twice at their insistence. It may be, of course, that he was anxious to quit, and used their advice as an excuse to back out without giving the appearance of fright.

He is a good historian, and gives a well-organized account of the progression of events in his life. One can see him watching the "head of the family" plant his squash seeds, and then secretly imitating him; or lying back in the hogan, speculating on why the method was successful.

He observes carefully and makes comparisons—the change in the weather since he was young, the deplorable state of the younger generation, the slackness of the modern dayschool as contrasted to the military type of boarding school he attended. He has opinions on everything, and in stating them shows his similarity to people of his age in our own society, who continually talk of the "good old days," and disapprove of things that are different.

Throughout his story shines a sense of humor and an alertness that are not so evident in the other two characters. His concluding sentence sums up his present state of contentment:

"I am in my home, inside where it is warm, and take care of all my property."

LOOKING FORWARD

WE ARE AT WAR now and the world's millions are suffering. One may ask of what significance is the health, the security, or the fate of the Navahos in the face of such vast issues. What matter the 50,000 Navahos, or the 370,000 Indians, in comparison with the 130 million people of the United States? Still less, what do they matter in comparison to the population of the world engaged in the present struggle?

What is one brick in a wall? What is one plate in a battleship? Perhaps they are indicators of the quality of other bricks and other plates.

The Indians are a small group among the 30 or more minority peoples who are part of the United States. There are 12 million negroes; 4 million Jews; a million and a half Canadians, Czechs, and Swedes; 5 million Italians; 3 million Poles; and several hundreds of thousands of Norwegians, Danes, French, Swiss, Russians, Greeks, and Finns, to name a few.* America has high ideals concerning such peoples and there are laws and articles in the Constitution to give these ideals form. Probably no country has better laws. In practice,

---

* Figures taken from Our Racial and National Minorities. Edited by Francis J. Brown and Joseph Slabey Roucek. N. Y. Prentice-Hall 1937.

however, we have in many instances failed to live up to these principles as we failed to live up to the 18th amendment while it existed.

This is a matter of no small importance for the future security of every man, woman, and child in the whole 130 millions of us. We are not in a position to decide whether or not we wish to be a nation derived from many cultures. We are such a nation and we contain such people in very great numbers. The only thing we can decide is whether or not the relations between these people are to be well or poorly handled, whether there will be strength built on integration, like a wall of bricks bound with cement, or whether we shall have weakness from internal conflict and social disorganization. Plywood, as long as the glue holds, is stronger than any solid plank of the same thickness, but once the glue begins to give way, it is weak and easily splintered.

The Nahavos represent one specific and concrete sample of our national policy in dealing with people across cultural boundaries. What we do to them is a test of our ability to live up to our principles and as such has bearing on the position of all other minorities. It is also an opportunity to learn, to establish better principles and set better precedents. It is equally an opportunity to fail ignominiously and show that our ideals and our capacity for fulfillment are far apart. At the present moment, this is not an idle and speculative question. While Navahos are fighting in the armed forces for a nation that does not allow them to vote, powerful movements are on foot to break treaty agreements and to open the way for taking their land and exploiting their labor.

If this nation is to be strong, it must have integrity in its dealings with minority peoples. This means being responsible for promises given and policies previously adopted, even when they have been made by a different Administration, a different Congress, a different political party, and even when they cost money. Circumstances change and promises and treaties have to be modified to meet the new conditions, but arbitrary changes, and changes based on the maneuvers of pressure groups to take away the Indians' possessions must be avoided. Few things have done more to undermine the Indians' morale than the history of unpredictable policy change which has marked our administration for many years. Things have been better since the Indian Reorganization Act, but at present they show a tendency to lapse again under the stimulus of a reactionary Congress.

We must have consistency in our dealings with minorities for the sake of our own lives and the lives of generations to come. Otherwise minor splits, rowdyism and local race riots will spread to larger disturbances; and issues between religious, economic, social, and geographic groups will become involved till the resulting confusion suggests the Balkan states rather than the United States.

Consistency can only be achieved if we curb those who will always seek to exploit minority peoples for their labor, or for their possessions. We cannot shout loudly about equality of opportunity for all, and at the same time have rigid local laws of discrimination, written and unwritten. We cannot fill minority peoples with promises one year and forget them the next. Most of all, we cannot permit private individuals, corporations, counties, or states to exploit minority people any more than we can permit them to waste and destroy for their own gain any other natural resource that belongs to the whole nation—any more than we can permit them to interfere with national security by placing obstacles in the way of the military forces.

Not all the dangers which threaten the adequate integration of minority peoples comes from this predatory activity of a few individuals and the indifference of the mass. Equally disturbing is the tendency to allow reactions from frustrations and irritations of life to focus on minorities as scapegoats. In times like the present, this danger is especially pressing. The predatory ones find it easy to whip up sympathy for their aims.

It may be argued that these things are deplorable, but that they are human nature and like sin and bad weather will be always with us. To this one can reply that at one time the same attitude was held toward plague and smallpox. Human history is the progress of the modification of human nature so that man can live more richly with his fellow men. Probably ever since man first acquired the use of speech the fatal fixity of human nature has been the excuse for avoid-

Navaho "Two-Seater," a Common Method of Transportation

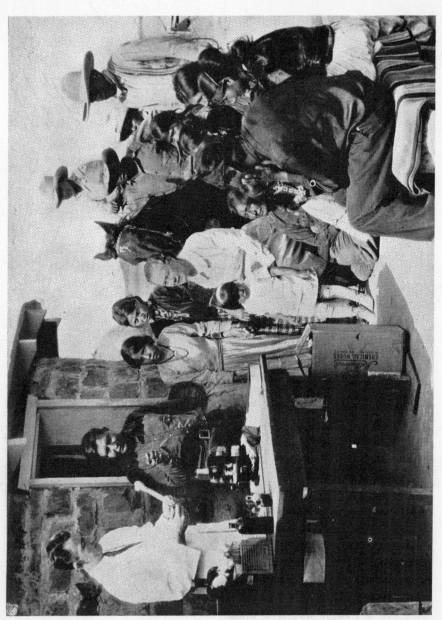

Teaching Navahos about Germs

ing the exertion involved in attempts at adjustment. Fifty years ago
human nature was the basis for depriving women of the vote and
of executive office. There is no reason today why the social liability
of prejudice—pre-judging, judging without waiting to ascertain
the facts—should not also be modified.

What is needed is that each and every one of us pay close attention to our Government, at least as close as those who have particular axes to grind. Democracy is founded as much on individual obligation to participate as it is on the rights and freedom of the individual. Neglect of this responsibility leads from democracy to what
Thomas Carlyle called "Quackocracy."

The authors are not trying to say that all peoples are the same.
It is obvious that there are in the world very wide cultural differences
between peoples, and a good deal of this book has been devoted to
describing some of the differences between the Navahos' way and
our own. Although there is no scientific evidence that differences are
constitutional, it is true that by the time a person is an adult he is so
conditioned to the patterns and attitudes of his culture that subsequent complete change is unlikely.

What we wish to emphasize is the need for stressing the common
ground between peoples, and the enlargement of that ground. Differences should be comprehended and adjusted, not magnified. Starting with our own cultural biases, we should be willing to meet people of other cultures half way, and not insist that they make all the
effort. With such an attitude and such a policy carried out con-
sistently, not only can we have much more national strength and
unity, but we can also add the contributions of these various cultures
to our progress and development.

What has been said about different kinds of peoples within our
nation is equally pertinent to our international relationships. The
very principles for which we are fighting are involved. We cannot
hope to be on proper terms with Russians, Argentinians, Peruvians,
British, and Chinese, if we are unable to understand the cultural
groups who are much more easily within the range of our compre-
hension. We must utilize the experience we have with the minorities inside our boundaries and apply the general principles deduced

therefrom across cultural lines outside the nation. Among the first of these is the requirement that we be reliable and willing to understand. Otherwise strong nations will regard us with mistrust and will play power politics, and weaker nations will look on us with sulky apathy, like a child who has capricious parents, and all together we will blunder along until the next conflagration.

There is no use lulling ourselves with songs about peace all over the world when the lights go on again if we do not realize that reliability and a capacity to understand apply all over the world. Otherwise, the only light that will go on will be the glow from burning civilization.

In conclusion, let us look once more at the Navahos. Let us look at a scene that is specific, yet general.

It is a warm day in midsummer and among the purple beeweed near a pinyon wood a dozen humming birds hover. From a Navaho hogan on a hill smoke rises, faint to see against the blue, but redolent with cedar smell even where invisible. Inside, a woman of about forty-five makes fried bread and peacefully gazes out the door where a trail winds over sage and sand till it vanishes around the flank of Flat Rock Mesa. Her sixteen-year-old son sits on a box mending harness. Her father, an old man with white hair on his shoulders and a mustache and goatee like Buffalo Bill lies on his back, a red handkerchief around his head and moccasins on his feet. He is sleeping off the effects of several days in town and some gallons of wine and dreaming of the Apache wars when he was a scout for the Army. Hanging from a nail on a beam behind the woman's head is a photograph in a cheap heart-shaped frame showing an Indian boy in the uniform of a Marine.

Outside the hogan two children, a boy and a girl, are playing at building a sheep corral in the wood-pile. By the red wheels of a green farm wagon with a white cover a black kitten moves like a free-lancing shadow.

A Navaho man, about the same age as the woman, rides slowly up on a pony with large bundles tied to his saddle. He brings the bundles into the hogan after freeing his animal, and the children come in from the wood-pile to see what he has fetched from the trader. The old man wakes up and joins the woman and older boy in waiting quietly to hear what news he has. They speak, of course, in Navaho.

"Where is Pauline?"

"She went out to get some yucca root to wash her hair. She should be back pretty soon."

"On my way back I met Red Salt's Son who was coming up from Shonto. He had a piece of yellow paper for me."

He takes a telegram out of his pocket and smoothing out the creases studies its transparent window while the others look on.

"Red Salt's Son said the man told him that it was from the Government for me. I want Pauline to read it and tell me what it says."

"She will be in soon," his wife says again. He folds the envelope carefully and thrusts it into an inner pocket, and lights a cigarette. He looks at the others and smiles.

"Maybe it doesn't say much."

After a pause he continues, "From what I heard at the trader's there hasn't been any rain around this country at all. Clouds and wind every afternoon, but rain no place. I don't know what we'll do next year if the ground doesn't get some water in it soon. No snow last winter and no rain this summer."

The old man begins rolling a cigarette and says, "Maybe the Government will give some help to the Indian."

"Maybe they would, but from what I hear it is more likely that they won't. They have no money for Indians, they say." He glances up at the picture of the young Marine.

"They won't keep the roads up much this winter, they have closed down Many Farms and two of the dayschools. They are short of doctors and it sounds as if they had no nurses at all. I guess the Indian will have to get along the best he can. But it is pretty hard with no help. There are more besides us with the young men gone away and no one to herd the sheep, haul the wood and water, and raise corn. We are in hard times and it looks to me as if they were getting worse. The Government has no money and is short of help, the year is drier than ever before and all the strong men are either fighting or in Flagstaff or some other place where there is a lot of war work."

The old man takes the cigarette out of his mouth and says, "When I was in town I heard some fellow say that they were going to close up the Indian Service and turn this land open to white cattle men. Did you hear anything about that?"

"The trader said he had heard some talk like that, but he didn't know whether to believe it or not."

The woman has been looking out the hogan door for some time, letting her eyes follow the trail by the mesa and now and then straying to the distant rim of Black Mountain.

"When Robert went off down that trail to join the Marines he said he was glad of a chance to get in the fight."

She looks at the old man and smiles.

"He tried to tell me where the fighting was and what it was about, but I couldn't understand except that it is away off that way across a lot of water. He talked a lot about the reason for the fight, things he said he learned in school. There was something in it about how the white man and the Indians were fighting now for the same things."

She turns a piece of bread over and pats it.

"It seemed to me that a young fellow just naturally wants to get where there is fighting and excitement."

She looks at the sixteen-year-old boy, who keeps his eyes on the harness.

"But I think he believed that after the war is over the white people and the Indians will get along together better. He seemed to think that while he was away fighting the Government would take care of his people back here at home, no matter how bad the times get. Then when he comes home at the end of the war, he thought that all the Navaho boys who had been fighting could pull together and get things better for the Indian because they had been fighting for the country. I remember one time he said, 'That is what this fight is all about.' I don't know, maybe he was right."

"He was in the army fifty years ago," says her husband with a look toward the old man, "I was in the last war 25 years ago, and now Robert is in this one. Maybe it helps, maybe it doesn't."

They all sit silent for a while, looking out the door at the Navaho country and at the trail through the sand and sage.

"I hope he isn't away too long," she says.

Her husband reaches forward to strike a match for a cigarette and the telegram crackles in his pocket. He wishes Pauline would come soon and tell him what it says. It may have something to do with reducing his herd of sheep still more.

He does not yet know that it is one of those telegrams that begin "The Navy Department deeply regrets to inform you that your son——"

NAVAHO KINSHIP TERMS

As SUGGESTED on page 23, the terms denoting various degrees of kinship are worth some study by workers among the Navaho, in order
to be able to get a clearer idea of the family make-up for medical
histories or school records. For this reason there is appended here a
list of the commonest and most important relationship terms, num-
bered for convenience of reference.

1. *Shimá,* my mother
2. *Shizhé'é,* my father
3. *Shádí,* my older sister
4. *Shideezhí,* my younger sister
5. *Sitsilí,* my younger brother
6. *Shínaaí,* my older brother
7. *Shidá'i,* my mother's brother
8. *Shik'á'í,* my mother's sister
9. *Shibizhí,* {my father's brother or sister (in preceding generation) / my brother's children (in following generation)}
10. *Shida',* my sister's son (man speaking)
11. *Shida'aké,* my nephew an dniece (man speaking)
12. *Shimá yázhí,* my sister's daughter (man speaking)
13. *Shizeedí,* my female cross-cousin (i. e., mother's brother's daugh-
     ter or father's sister's daughter)
14. *Shiłnaa'aash,* my male cross-cousin
15. *Shik'éi,* my relatives
16. *Shichai,* my mother's father
17. *Shichó,* my mother's mother's mother (sometimes locally used
     for my mother's mother)
18. *Shimá sání,* my mother's mother
19. *Shitsóí,* my daughter's child
20. *Shináli,* my son's children (also used for my father's father and
     my father's mother)

21. *Shahastiin*, my husband
22. *She'esdzą́ą́*, my wife
23. *Shighe*, my son (man speaking)
24. *Shiyáázh*, my son (woman speaking)
25. *Shitsi'*, my daughter (man speaking)
26. *Shich'é'é*, my daughter (woman speaking)

The prefix *si-* or *shi-* means "my," and can be replaced by *ni-* for "your," or by *bi-* for "his" or "her." This list is not exhaustive, but will serve as a starter and will probably be sufficient for most purposes.

Examination of the list brings to one's attention a number of contrasts between English and Navaho kinship terms. In the first place, age in relation to the speaker is often shown as can be seen in 3-6. Next, relationship through the father's or mother's line is distinguished, as is evident in 7-9, 16, and 20. The sex of the speaker makes a difference in the word chosen, as can be seen in 10, 11, 12, and 23-26. Finally, the same term may be used to denote people in the generation before and the generation after the speaker. One fact that does not appear from this list is that the same term may be used for several different relationships, as, for instance, *shimá*, which may mean "my real mother," "my mother's or father's sister," "woman in my mother's generation who is in my clan," or merely a term of respect for an older woman.

It is also quite apparent that the Navahos do not say "Uncle" or "Aunt" or "Cousin" in the general sense that we do, and if a relationship is so designated by an interpreter it is best to ask what word is used by the two parties when they speak to each other. For instance, if two men call each other *"shináli,"* it is quite sure that one is grandson and the other grandfather. Similarly, if two men call each other *"shida'"* and *"shidá'í,"* respectively, they are uncle and nephew through the younger man's mother.

BIBLIOGRAPHY

IN THIS LIST of books and articles from journals, no attempt has been made to include all the writings read by the authors in preparing this book. Rather, we have tried to indicate sources which would probably be both interesting and valuable to readers if they wish more detail than has been included in the preceding chapters. For a list of books concerning the Navahos, complete to its date of publication, readers are referred to Kluckhohn and Spencer's *A Bibliography of the Navaho Indians,* which came out in 1940 (New York).

Adair, John: *The Navajo and Pueblo Silversmiths* (in preparation).
Amsden, Charles A.: "Navaho Origins," *New Mexico Historical Review,* VII: 193-209 (1932).
  Navaho Weaving, Its Technic and History (Santa Ana, California, 1934). 261 pages. Illustrated.
Coolidge, Dane: *Lorenzo the Magnificent* (New York, 1925). 320 pages.
— Coolidge, Dane, and Coolidge, Mary R.: *The Navajo Indians* (Boston, 1930). 309 pages.
Dyk, Walter: *Son of Old Man Hat, a Navajo Autobiography* (New York, 1938). 378 pages.
Franciscan Fathers: *An Ethnologic Dictionary of the Navaho Language* (St. Michaels, Arizona, 1910). 536 pages.
Gilmor, Frances, and Wetherill, Louisa W.: *Traders to the Navajos* (Boston, 1934). 265 pages.
Hill, Willard W.: *The Agricultural and Hunting Methods of the Navaho Indians* (Yale University Publications in Anthropology 18, 1938). 194 pages. Illustrated.
La Farge, Oliver: *Laughing Boy* (Boston, 1929). 302 pages.
Luomala, Katherine: *Navaho Life of Yesterday and Today* (U. S. Department of the Interior, National Park Service, Berkeley, California, 1938). 115 pages. Mimeographed.

Morris, Anne A.: *Digging in the Southwest* (Garden City, New York, 1933).

Newcomb, Franc J., and Reichard, Gladys A.: *Sand Paintings of the Navajo Shooting Chant* (New York, 1937). 87 pages. 35 plates.

Reichard, Gladys A.: *Navajo Shepherd and Weaver* (New York, 1936). 222 pages. Illustrated.

Van Valkenburgh, Richard F.: "Navajo Common Law I: Notes on Political Organization, Property and Inheritance," Museum of Northern Arizona, *Museum Notes*, IX: 17-22 (1936).

"Navajo Common Law II: Navajo Law and Justice," *Idem*, IX: 51-54 (1937).

"Navajo Common Law III: Etiquette, Hospitality, Justice," *Idem*, X: 39-45 (1938).

Wyman, Leland C.: "Navaho Diagnosticians," *American Anthropologist*, XXXVIII: 236-246 (1936).

INDEX